Managing Very Challenging Behaviour

Continuum International Publishing Group
The Tower Building, 11 York Road, London, SE1 7NX
80 Maiden Lane, Suite 704, New York, NY 10038

www.continuumbooks.com

British Library Cataloguing-in-Publication Data
A catalogue record for this book is available from the British Library.

ISBN: 978-0-8264-3877-5 (paperback)

Library of Congress Cataloging-in-Publication Data
Leaman, Louisa.
  Managing very challenging behaviour / Louisa Leaman. — 2nd ed.
    p. cm.
  ISBN 978-0-8264-3877-5 (pbk.)
1. School discipline. 2. Classroom management. 3. Problem children—
Behavior modification. I. Title.

  LB3012.L43 2009
  371.5—dc22
  2009001596

Designed and typeset by Kenneth Burnley, Wirral, Cheshire
Printed and bound in Great Britain by Ashford Colour Press Ltd,
Gosport, Hants.

Managing
Very Challenging
Behaviour

2nd edition

LOUISA LEAMAN

continuum

Continuum International Publishing Group
The Tower Building, 11 York Road, London, SE1 7NX
80 Maiden Lane, Suite 704, New York, NY 10038

www.continuumbooks.com

British Library Cataloguing-in-Publication Data
A catalogue record for this book is available from the British Library.

ISBN: 978-0-8264-3877-5 (paperback)

Library of Congress Cataloging-in-Publication Data
Leaman, Louisa.
  Managing very challenging behaviour / Louisa Leaman. — 2nd ed.
    p. cm.
  ISBN 978-0-8264-3877-5 (pbk.)
1. School discipline. 2. Classroom management. 3. Problem children—Behavior modification. I. Title.

  LB3012.L43 2009
  371.5—dc22
  2009001596

Designed and typeset by Kenneth Burnley, Wirral, Cheshire
Printed and bound in Great Britain by . . .

Contents

Introduction

Managing challenging students within the educational setting is not a new problem, neither is it a problem that is going to go away. As teaching professionals, we may hate the fact that every time we get the class going, the rat-faced boy with ADHD oozing from his fingertips starts using his ruler as a missile launcher. We may feel aggrieved by the blatant lack of courtesy displayed by a group of 15-year-olds, who act as though we have mortally offended them by asking for quiet. We may be intimidated by the undercurrent of menace that lurks in the corridors, the possibility of a fight erupting outside our classroom door. We may well feel frustrated – we came to this profession to *teach*, not control crowds.

So we find ourselves regularly battling against frustrating, disruptive, hostile and sometimes disturbing behaviour, yet this role is secondary to our real intended purpose: learning. There is no denying that teaching is a tough job. Trying to inspire and inform young minds while managing difficult classroom behaviour is a huge bite to chew. But it can be made easier if we know how to manage challenging students with confidence and skill. Having this knowledge will not eradicate behavioural problems, nor will it reduce the workload, but it can enable us to minimize the impact of difficulties, maintain a positive learning environment and keep our stress levels in check. Whether we like it or not, challenging behaviour is here to stay. If we acknowledge its presence, develop the skills to manage it, and learn to work *with* it, we enable ourselves to maintain control and move forward.

With limited time and enormous pressures we may well resent spending time dealing with behavioural issues. Unfortunately behavioural issues, by their very nature, require exactly those things: time and patience. This book provides practical, workable advice to teachers trying to combat this issue, and will hopefully ensure that any attention given to behaviour problems is productive and worthwhile. I discuss strategies that encourage long-term progress and seek changes in student attitude, as opposed to simply punishing the immediate problem. If we are to really address challenging behaviour, we need to do more than just punish it. We need to understand its existence, and then challenge it from that basis.

Something I always say to teachers who come to me for advice and training is that the starting point should always be asking 'Why'. Why are students misbehaving? What are their motivations? What are their triggers? Are they bored? Are they looking for attention? Are they insecure about their abilities? Do they have a 'bad' reputation to protect? Have they been up all night on their PlayStations, drinking vodka and Red Bull? Do their parents seem remotely concerned about their academic performance?

Reasons for behaviour difficulties are as diverse as the students themselves. The process of getting to know why students misbehave is about getting to know the students themselves. It may, from time to time, require a bit of self reflection too. Is there something that you, as the teacher, can develop or change to help ease problems? For example, rethinking tasks/teaching methods to make them more accessible, or adapting your manner during confrontations. What happens in the classroom is not just about what the student does, but what the teacher does as well.

This is not a book that seeks to blame poor student behaviour on weak teaching however, but one that offers a tool of reflection, enabling teachers to maximize their skills and make their classroom work for them. Also, my intention is not to take a soft approach to disruption, in the 'poor dears, they can't help it – they've had tough lives' mode. When I encourage teachers to consider why their students misbehave, I am asking them to look for explanations, *not* excuses!

Personally, I believe effective behaviour management should encourage students to take responsibility for their actions, no matter what their circumstances are. It is about supporting students to manage their own behaviour: learning to get control of themselves, as opposed to the teacher taking control for them. Hence I emphasize responsibility and making choices. For some students, being responsible and recognizing the effect of their actions can seem like an alien concept – those who are quick to misbehave, but not so quick to admit to it: 'It wasn't me Miss.' No. It was that boy that always sits next to you, the invisible one . . .

The ideas in this book are based on my own experiences of working with challenging students in both special and mainstream settings, at primary and secondary level. Working as an Advisory

Behaviour Support Teacher, Trainer and Behaviour Coordinator I have had the opportunity to observe exactly what goes on between teachers and their students. I have seen the frustration, the stress and the disappointment that challenging behaviour can bring to a classroom – but I have also seen triumphant examples of positive intervention. I have come to realize that, while there are many different types of teacher and many different types of behaviour, there are certain skills and approaches that are common to all those who succeed with behaviour management. It is these insights that I wish to share.

I learned the hard way – taking tough jobs, in tough schools, in tough boroughs – with limited training and little idea of what I was letting myself in for! I struggled at first and made a few mistakes; but for this I am glad, because it taught me so much. Getting to grips with behaviour management is a process; it relies on practice, experience and reflection. But if we are prepared to invest some energy and commitment into developing this process, we can challenge the challenge with confidence.

1 | Overview

This is not a book about general classroom behaviour management. It focuses specifically on dealing with the high end of challenging behaviour, and explores ways of working with the kind of student who exhibits this behaviour: the kind of student who is often preceded by his or her reputation, known for the ability to destroy well-planned lessons in a matter of seconds.

Throughout this book I will make reference to students with emotional, social and behavioural difficulties (ESBD). This description is used to define a sector of students identified as having special educational needs (SEN). In order to be granted this acronym, a student would need to have a Statement of SEN, or be on the way to receiving one. This is not to say that the only students who will exhibit challenging behaviour are those who are Statemented; or that Statemented pupils will necessarily be the source of all your problems, but it is this level of challenge that I will be focusing on.

Working in special schools and units for students with ESBD, I have encountered the extreme end of the problem. I have been kicked, punched, head-butted, strangled, spat at, sworn at and called names so rude l would not dare write them down . . . *but* in between those 'difficult' moments I have seen students succeed and make progress, both educationally and socially, in ways that have sometimes surprised and impressed me. In ESBD education the rewards can seem scarce, but when they do arise, they are very worthwhile. This environment has taught me the value of empathy: to see beyond undesirable behaviour, to recognize the damaged individual behind the outrageous act. It has also taught me to never, ever take things personally. However, working with ESBD students in small-group settings, with intensive support, a heavy emphasis on social skills and a carefully adapted curriculum, is an entirely different experience from educating such students in a mainstream setting.

Within the current climate of *inclusive* education, mainstream schools may have a number of students with SENs. It is very likely that some of these will have ESBD. It is not so likely (but perhaps it is sod's law) that every one of them will be in your form group. You have a class of 30 mixed-ability 11-year-olds. Some of them are really bright. Some of them could do well, given the right amount of nurturing. A couple of them are loudmouths who need a daily reminder about the purpose of school. A few of them are quiet, alarmingly so. One of them has mobility problems . . . but you apply most of your efforts to dealing with the three who spend more time in detention than they do in lessons. The three who seem to be permanently on report, who never get to class on time, never hand in homework and are often seen rolling around in the dirt with a group of angry 15-year-olds. They are also the three most likely to have connections with the ESBD underworld. If we've all got something to say about the decline of youth behaviour, we've probably got something to say about the realities of inclusion.

I have seen many examples of challenging students being successfully integrated into mainstream lessons, but I have also seen the strain and pressure that this can place upon a school and its staff. I have watched an individual student run rings around a group of experienced senior teachers. I have listened to strong, competent practitioners despairing of the daily belligerence they find themselves facing. And I have consoled a number of stressed-out new teachers who have reached breaking point all too early in their careers. I hope that this book will bring comfort and inspiration to anyone who feels that they need to reclaim their classroom!

Two factors that I want to briefly consider are, firstly, the differences between primary and secondary teaching. I have worked in both sectors and believe that the advice in this book has universal relevance, although some aspects and examples may be more appropriate to younger/older students. In all instances, however, you, the reader/teacher, will know your students better than me, so you are in the best position to decide what will have an impact on them – I have encountered teachers who say their hardened teenagers melt at the sight of a reward sticker, and others who say they've long grown out of them. Likewise, some primary school teachers swear by getting students to solve their silly squabbles amongst themselves; others get results by guiding them through the process step-by-step.

From my own experience, the two sectors do present different challenges. Many of these are to do with differing systems and structures within the schools themselves. Primary schools tend to have a greater capacity for 'nurture': a group of students together in one class, with (hopefully) one main teacher, for the entire year. Strong relationships can be forged and the environment is generally secure and familiar. When considering behaviour, this has obvious benefits: a greater level of consistency can be achieved, and teachers have enough contact time with students to be able to really 'mould' them.

On the other hand, if the chemistry between the students and the teacher is off, it can lead to a tough few terms. Similarly, if there are rivalries or socialization issues between groups of students, it can create considerable problems, which start to feel inescapable as the year rolls on. In this respect, the secondary system has its benefits. Different lessons with different teachers, and often different mixes of students, allows for flexibility and 'breathing room'. The down side, of course, is that the sense of familiarity and nurture slips away (which, for some volatile secondary pupils, can be a coping disaster), and consistency of input is harder to achieve (different teachers having different levels of expectation), not to mention the challenge of having an influence over, and keeping track of, students who may sit in your classroom for no more than an hour a week.

Second, I wish to highlight an issue that often rears its head when matters of inclusion/challenging behaviour are being discussed. What do you do when, despite your best efforts, your school/managers/behaviour policy are not helping or supporting you? Unfortunately there is no simple answer to this problem (although the defeatist in me wants to say 'leave'!). There are schools out there, however, that do seem to be getting it right, not just for the students but for the staff as well. The thing they have in common is a positive, realistic 'can-do' ethos that all staff, at all levels, embrace – and they embrace it because they know that if there are problems, they will be listened to. That management value them and understand the challenges they face.

I sometimes hear stories about crazy or inflexible policy decisions: teachers not being allowed to contact parents, line pupils up in corridors, give out detentions, or use the word 'good'! Problems often stem not from the policies themselves, but from the way in which they are established. In order to be meaningful and effective, policies have to be written in consultation with the people they relate to: the staff, the pupils, and even the parents. Teachers working on the front line need to have a say in what works and what doesn't, as they will be the ones putting it to effect. There also need to be regular opportunities to review how things are going and, if necessary, make changes. Schools that succeed are not afraid of admitting when things aren't working, and when they do work, they don't rest on their laurels, but keep upping their game.

2 | Why pupils misbehave

Making sense of senseless behaviour: the underlying issues of challenge in the classroom

There is no such thing as evil. Youth behaviour that challenges the common expectations and values of society is not the result of inherent wickedness, but is a multi-faceted problem emerging from a complex network of factors. Simplistic, sensationalist media hype (blame 'computer games', blame 'hamburgers', blame 'weak school discipline', blame 'illegal immigrants') confuses the issue, but rarely recognizes the whole picture: the roots of challenging behaviour are embedded in our entire social fabric. If we want to change behaviour, we have to change everything: no quick fixes.

So we all have a responsibility to face up to society's ills – whether we do is another matter. Those of us that make the choice to work in education, like it or not, assume an especially significant role in addressing social decline. We nurse the casualties of human nature's ineptness: youth. Reception children having violent outbursts. Year 4s using foul language we never knew existed. An entire Year 6 class victimizing one individual. Year 7s dealing drugs in the playground. A Year 9 student punching a classroom assistant. Year 10s missing weeks of schooling at a time. Year 11 gangs terrorizing the corridors. Where does this come from if it does not come from the 'evil' gene?

An underlying theme of the advice given in this book is *awareness*. If we know what we are dealing with, we are better able to deal with it. A school sometimes seems like a microcosm of its wider community. Its successes and struggles are bound by the social, cultural and environmental contexts from which it emerges. Maybe there are economic factors affecting the surrounding area: unemployment, lack of affordable housing, low incomes? What is the local community like? Are there any positive aspirations for the future? Are there any issues with drug/alcohol abuse? Dysfunctional families? Low levels of adult literacy? Lack of local amenities? Inappropriate peer influences?

Time and time again, I look into the backgrounds and life circumstances of my ESBD students, and it starts to make sense. Deprivation. Lack of consistent nurture. Lack of familial stability. Lack of appropriate role models (particularly male). Exposure to violence. Experience of physical, sexual or emotional abuse. Inappropriate living conditions. These are just a handful of the variables.

Without wishing to scapegoat parents, special attention must be paid to the distinct influence they have on their offspring's ability to function in the rigours of wider society. Lack of boundaries, inadequate parenting skills, abuse, neglect and inconsistency are just some of the circumstances that can contribute to a young persons impaired emotional and social development. It is no wonder that the child who has experienced little structure, guidance or balanced discipline in their young life will struggle to relate to the order of the classroom.

Add to this, the numbers of young people identified as having medical/cognitive issues: ADHD, ADD, autistic spectrum disorders, anxiety disorders, attachment disorders, and depression. And, of course, the issue of learning needs, specific (dyslexia, dyspraxia and dyscalculia) or otherwise. If left undetected, learning problems can give rise to behavioural problems: the frustration and embarrassment of not 'getting it' like everyone else. On the other hand, behavioural problems can significantly disrupt learning: difficulties concentrating, truancy, and a heightened state of agitation are not conducive to the absorption of knowledge. Delayed learning simply makes it harder to tolerate the experience of school.

Behaviour may also be affected by the sporadic situations that can occur in a young person's life: arguments with friends, difficulties at home, bereavement – temporary problems that can see a change in an individual's manner or an increase in anger. ESBD has varied origins, and often evolves from a combination of factors. There is no simple solution: removing a child from an abusive household and placing them in care brings a new set of problems. Courses to improve parenting skills are useful, but only if ideas are taken on board. Counselling/anger management has its place, but not if the child refuses to participate. Moreover, ESBD has a stigma attached to it: 'anti-social' does not often invoke a sympathetic response.

I am not making excuses for challenging behaviour – I simply wish to rationalize it. I am aware that many people grow up within traumatic circumstances, and develop into fine, well-adjusted members of society. So why do some individuals feel the need to go around trashing classrooms, swearing at teachers and generally giving authority the finger? Each person is different, and will interpret their circumstances in a way that is personal to them. The ability to thrive through adversity is dependent on many factors: the personality of the individual, the support and guidance they have received, and their capacity for intellectual and emotional understanding. For some, the combination of internal and external circumstances will manifest itself as emotional/behavioural difficulties, or what could also be thought of as misguided coping mechanisms.

An emotional issue: the hidden agendas of troubled individuals

As a teacher, you may encounter a range of complications arising from ESBD. Some of these will be observable behaviours, some will be emotional issues. There may also be concerns about health and welfare. For the purposes of this book, I will be focusing on how to manage the actual behaviour, but wish to stress that emotional development (and physical welfare) is intrinsically linked to this. It is hard to make progress in one area without being mindful of the others. Thus, I wish to highlight some of the emotional issues that may underlie challenging behaviour. At the risk of over-simplifying the case, I am focusing on three key areas: low self-esteem, egocentricity and internalized anger. I have chosen these because they have been the most prevalent in my experience.

Low self-esteem

Students who have missed out on stable, nurturing home environments may have a very poor self-image. This can be obvious: the student that always says they 'can't do it'. Or it can be concealed: the student with lots of bravado, the leader of the pack, the show-off, the bully – may well be overcompensating for deep insecurities. Students with self-esteem issues may lack aspirations and motivation: the 'lazy' ones. Work output could be poor, because of real or perceived difficulties. Tasks may not get started due to fear of failure. Students that are struggling in school (be it through their behaviour or learning) may have a bleak outlook on themselves and their situation. Unfortunately, this becomes a vicious cycle, reinforced by the negative labels that are often attached to difficult students (not just from schools, but other arenas of society: 'the problem child', 'the troublemaker', 'the irritating little ****').

I have seen students become so heavily weighted with low self-esteem that they fail to accept their successes, even when they are pointed out to them. Low self-esteem relates to feelings of inadequacy. Feelings of inadequacy lead to anxieties about status and acceptance. These anxieties can translate into power-seeking behaviour. Students that dominate the classroom, refuse to follow instructions and ridicule or confront others, may be desperate to prove themselves. Fear is the common thread. Fear of losing. Fear of not being liked or loved. Fear of not being noticed. Fear of not being accepted. Fear of losing control or of others taking control. Fear of violence. Fear of the unpredictable. Fear of being weak. Fear of change.

Egocentricity

Think of the student who seems to delight in winding up his class-mates. He knows how to do it with just a look. When your back is turned he mouths crude insults at his target – he usually goes for the student he knows will react badly. He does it time and time again, despite ending up in countless fights, losing popularity and gaining detentions. One of the most common difficulties exhibited by students with ESBD is a limited repertoire of social skills. Difficulties empathizing with the feelings and needs of the people around them, combined with underlying anger and insecurity, can lead to in-appropriate ways of seeking attention, and what may seem like a compulsion to insult, belittle and aggravate others. This behaviour is complex and difficult to solve – it may be unappealing, but it requires some understanding. In a crude expression: people make others suffer, because they are suffering themselves.

I use the term 'egocentricity' because behaviour of this kind often seems self-absorbed. Students will rarely recognize or identify with how their behaviour affects others. They will be preoccupied with their own drives and needs, and will pursue these at any cost. Such individuals may show little remorse for their actions, or fail to modify their behaviour – they fail to truly connect to the way in which it hurts or upsets others. Other facets of egocentric activity include poor listening skills, emotional immaturity, manipulative behaviour, the avoidance of responsibility, a strong sense of justice and a need to control others/be dominant.

Internalized anger

If a child has had difficult experiences in their life, and has not devel-oped the emotional capacity to process and cope efficiently with their feelings, they can harbour many negative internal responses:

shame, resentment, anger, frustration, fear, anxiety, confusion, insecurity, guilt. Without helpful channels of expression, these feelings can remain internalized and, often, unexplored. However, high levels of stress or tension have to come out somehow. Aggressive, controlling, bullying, unpredictable, high-tempered and obstructive behaviour vented on anyone or anything – think of the child that is commonly described as a 'time-bomb'. The anger may be intended for someone, or something, else, but perhaps this is not accessible, or not safe. Schools are perhaps a fairly safe place to express anger: there are people around who can take control, keep order and pick up the pieces.

Of course, not all pupils that exhibit disruptive behaviour will be angry about the world. Some of them will have solid, supportive upbringings. So what is their motivation? Some students will have medical/cognitive issues that will interfere with their school experience (for instance, hyperactivity disorders). Some will have an individual will or personality that leads them to vent their energies in this manner. Others will bow to social pressures to behave in certain ways. Image is so important to young people. We live in a culture that believes in winning through dominance: losing face with a teacher is not cool.

3 | The backbone of behaviour management

Key skills that every teacher should know about

This book provides guidance on methods for dealing with particular types of challenging behaviour, ranging from low-level disruption to violent assault. I wish to provide advice that is as relative as possible to specific problems, thus its application will be clear and instructive. However, it is perhaps useful to briefly clarify the key features of this advice: the basic principles of effective, meaningful behaviour management.

1 Assert clear boundaries.
2 Be consistent.
3 Use a sliding scale of intervention.
4 Give pupils a way out.
5 Provide meaningful rewards/consequences.
6 Reflect and learn from your own practice.
7 Build relationships with pupils.

Assert clear boundaries

Boundaries provide a sense of security, safety and stability, and they help to establish an understanding of acceptable and unacceptable behaviour. Ironically, some students may create challenge in order to reach a boundary – especially if this is something that is lacking in the rest of their life. Knowing you will be noticed and stopped can feel very reassuring. Though they may seem resistant to them at times, young people need and benefit from boundaries, but be prepared: putting together a 'class rules' poster is not enough, you need to be able to assert and stick by them no matter how hard students push.

◆ Think about what matters to you, your teaching style and the school's behaviour policy before meeting new classes. Get it clear in your own head, and then ensure that your students are aware of what is and is not expected of them – do not assume that they will know.

◆ Establish class rules/rights/boundaries at the start of term and continue to refer to them throughout the year. Re-establish them regularly in order to confirm their relevance and importance. Use them as your justification for discipline, or as a reminder/warning.

◆ Explain to your students why certain boundaries are necessary, and discuss the cause and effect of crossing these boundaries. Emphasizing the reasoning behind a code of conduct can make it more memorable and logical.

◆ There is nothing wrong with having high expectations, as long as they are achievable and regularly encouraged.

Be consistent

Consistency is vital in developing trust and compliance. If your responses to challenging behaviour are consistently calm, firm and thorough (i.e., you see things through), your students will recognize that you are able to remain in control of the classroom and that they will not get away with it (which may deter some of them). They will also see that you treat people fairly and are unlikely to react with sudden aggression or loss of temper (a red rag to an ESBD student!). Being consistent relies on you having a clear conception of how you deal with challenging behaviour: know what this is before problems arise. If necessary, anticipate certain responses and consequences to specific behaviours, so that they are at hand when you need them. There are always, of course, situations where flexibility is required, and for this you need to use common sense: Gary starts swearing at Leon because Leon has deliberately poured paint over Gary's best artwork. Should Gary receive a detention for use of offensive language? You may decide to moderate the consequence, given the context of the swearing – but remember, this may also need to be justified in the eyes of students who received detentions for verbal fouling last week. When tackling less straightforward issues of behaviour (for instance, arguments), make sure you get to the bottom of the problem before meting out consequences.

Use a sliding scale of intervention

Your emphasis should always be on diffusing a situation, ensuring it has the minimum of impact on yourself and your students. I know many teachers that are unflinchingly convinced that intimidating methods of behaviour control (such as aggressive shouting) are the most effective. For a selection of students I'm sure that they are, but in the inclusive classroom – where the mix of students may incorporate emotionally vulnerable, unstable individuals – this approach is outmoded. Scream at a young person with ESBD, and, unless you have a particularly strong relationship with them, the problem will probably escalate. It is important to intervene at the least intrusive level possible, and increase intensity as and when necessary. In other words, do not start yelling at a student (increasing the stress on yourself and the class), when a 'look' will do the job. If low-level interventions (a quiet word, a 'look', moving towards the problem) fail, go to the next level (raise your voice, issue a warning). This approach does not need to rely on prescriptive lists of what interventions should be used and when, but on your good judgement: your sense of what is needed and what your student's responses will be. Simply aim to manage a problem with as little fuss as possible every step of the way, calm, measured and neutral – drawing as little attention to the behaviour as possible. Heavy interventions, such as physical handling (restraining) or student removal should *always* be a last resort.

Give pupils a way out

One of the reasons why challenging behaviour can be so persistent is that young people are not recognizing (or are choosing to override), the cause and effect principle of life: if you behave like X, then Y will happen. When you challenge challenging behaviour, it is vital that you encourage your students to take responsibility for their actions, and recognize that there will be consequences to face up to. I have observed teachers who have enviably tight classroom control, but achieve this through holding frighteningly strict reins on their students (I would even suggest that students are intimidated (bullying by another name) into behaving themselves). From experience, I would surmise that this approach has limited benefit on an individual's long-term behavioural prospects: they are not learning to manage or have ownership over their own behaviour, someone else is managing it for them – what happens when that influence is taken away? Encouraging students to make their own choices over the outcome of events is an effective way of promoting accountability. If a student has a choice of actions and corresponding outcomes, the responsibility is theirs. The right choice leads to positive things; the wrong choice leads to negatives – it is up to them. Providing choice also offers a way out for the student, allowing them to retain control of their experience – which is particularly important when dealing with individuals who resent feeling cornered.

Ultimately, we cannot *force* our students to cooperate, whether it's for their own good or not, and trying to do so can easily lead to power battles and conflict. Take, for example, the students who chew gum as they walk into the classroom. Of course, the majority of them will put it in the bin when you remind them that it is against school rules. A few, however, will see this as an opportunity to challenge you and the system. If they refuse, what are you going to do? Hook your finger into their mouth and scoop the gum out yourself? Didn't think so. Choice makes everything seem more reasonable and less personal:

> 'Danny, you know the rule about chewing gum. Either it goes in the bin or I have to put you on a warning. Save yourself from trouble, eh?'

Meeting Danny halfway, by calmly offering him the waste paper bin, will also help to broker the deal, giving him the message that you are working with him, rather than against him.

Another way to diffuse potential conflict and encourage pupils to be responsible for their own actions and reactions is the use of 'time-out' (otherwise known as 'turn-around time', 'reflection time', 'taking five', etc.). It is important that consequences for challenging behaviour are not peddled as 'punishing wrongdoing', but as a way of resolving and owning up to problematic activity.

If an individual is encouraged to move away from a difficulty or conflict, it may prevent a situation from escalating further – removing the audience and giving them time to reflect or calm down. Moreover, it will give you time to compose yourself and focus on the rest of the class. Effective use of 'time-out', however, relies on a number of things: a suitable space in which it may be taken, student understanding of the process, and how you are able to follow it up.

Space is the key issue. A time-out chair or area provided 'in-class' is ideal in the first instance, particularly for younger students (older students may find it patronizing). However, if a child is having extreme difficulties, or is liable to continue to disrupt the lesson/be wound-up, it may be more suitable to send them outside the room. Once outside, they will be harder to monitor, and there is a risk that they will run away or disrupt other classes. Many schools have a policy in which difficult students can be sent to other classrooms to be 'minded' by fellow teachers. This can certainly solve the problem of accountability, but should not be over-relied on: you need to be seen to be dealing with behaviour yourself, in order to have your behaviour management believed in.

In an ideal world, I would advocate sending students to a chair outside the classroom door. Make it clear that this is not a punishment, but a chance for them to get their head together, work out what they need to do to put things right, and get themselves back into class with no more problems. After five minutes (or less, if appropriate), I would speak to them – assess their readiness to return to the lesson and establish the next steps (facing responsibility, making apologies, returning to class). Time-out should act as a buffer between difficult behaviour and its consequences: an opportunity for the individual to turn the situation around. It is vital that this is understood by the students themselves, otherwise they may be resistant to it or view it as a punishment. It is worth considering that students may, at times, decide to self-administer time-out (in other words, go without being asked). This I would encourage, as it promotes a mature inclination to avoid problematic situations – but make sure that it is not being abused (an excuse to get out of work). Time-out needs to be brief.

For more hardened offenders or persistent misbehaviour, time-out may have to take the form of a longer-lasting solution. Many schools have developed effective systems of temporary student withdrawal, either 'swapping' them into different classrooms for the remainder of the lesson, or sending them to a specified place – an office or staffed area set up to deal with disruptive students. This has the added benefit of giving you, the teacher, and the rest of the class a bit of breathing room.

Provide meaningful rewards/consequences

A powerful way of reinforcing how you want things to be in your classroom is by providing a clear and fair system of rewards and consequences. Not *punishments* – remember, this has negative connotations, but *consequences* – the resulting action of inappropriate behaviour. If the teacher response to appropriate/inappropriate behaviour is consistent, the student's potential to identify with the benefits of working within your boundaries will be maximized. If students are helpful they will receive all kinds of good things: regular praise and recognition being the most important. If they are unhelpful, they will have to make up for this somehow – at your convenience, not theirs. Rewards and consequences need to be meaningful, and simple to administer.

Rewards

Positive encouragement and praise is the easiest and most powerful way to reward an individual: notice your students working quietly/being helpful/listening well/sitting still, as much as you notice them misbehaving. Draw attention to this, and make them feel good about themselves. In addition, more tangible rewards may be useful. However, in a busy mainstream setting these can sometimes be difficult to keep track of. Keep it simple: stickers, certificates, merits or special incentives (a points chart leading to a goal – a treat at the end of the week, or some free time). In the past, I have found incentives that have immediate gratifying effect, little and often, are more successful than big long-term goals (which can be hard to believe in). As an example, every morning my students would work towards ten minutes' 'golden' time before break (a chance to choose an activity for themselves), if they worked particularly well they would gain extra minutes. They could also lose minutes for inappropriate behaviour. Importantly, they all began with the same amount of time. This reward system led to some very productive mornings.

Within a mainstream class environment, particularly challenging students may benefit from some personalized attention with regard to rewards. The fact is, it may not always be fair to measure their behaviour against the rest of their classmates: they are individuals with 'special' needs. Small, insignificant achievements may be massive successes in the context of their personal behaviour difficulties.

Consequences

If a student learns to take advantage of 'time-out', especially if it is used pre-emptively (before the behaviour becomes significantly problematic), they will hopefully recognize that walking away from a problem and calming down is a good way of avoiding negativity and consequence. However, I realize that despite good intentions,

challenging behaviour can escalate very quickly, or will be so immediately inappropriate that consequences are inevitable. There are
also people (particularly schoolchildren) who seem to want to see the
swift hand of justice administering 'punishment' – students are often
resentful of teachers that appear to allow individuals to get away
with 'bad' behaviour, and it is important that this viewpoint is
catered for. Use consequences with caution though. Your agenda
runs deeper: you don't (just) want to get revenge on those that
disrupt your lessons, you want them to change and develop them,
and give them the opportunity to make the best of themselves.
Consequences alone have limited meaningful effect on changing
behaviour – if they are effective, then why do so many people repeatedly behave in anti-social ways? When they are made use of, they
need to be meaningful, fair and issued out of rationality (rather than
anger). They also need to reflect the gravity of the problem – minor
incidents call for small consequences: short detentions, litter-picking,
catching up on work. Serious incidents may lead to phone-calls
home, involvement of senior staff or even exclusion. But, unless
efforts are also made to encourage students to take responsibility for
their actions, to recognize how their behaviour affects others, and to
want to engage with the classroom experience in positive ways –
consequences will have little impact.

Reflect and learn from your own practice

This book aims to provide help in the trickiest of moments, picking
up where day-to-day classroom management skills might finish.
However, dealing with particularly challenging behaviour is most
easily achieved in a classroom that is already established as a calm,
well-ordered and stable environment. It is important to develop a
general level of understanding and expectation between yourself
and all of your students: a solid platform for success. Of course, challenging students will not automatically toe the line if the rest of the
class do – but in a calm, teacher-defined environment it is far easier
to monitor and address obstructive behaviour and to feel in control
of the situation.

Teaching styles vary enormously, and bring with them varying
approaches to discipline. While consistency is important, it has to be
achieved within an allowance for different teacher styles and intentions. We do not all practise in the same way, nor should we – but
there are a few underlying principles of good living, let alone good
classroom practice, that can underline our personalized approach:

- Be firm.
- Be fair.
- Be calm.
- Be clear.
- Be positive.

At the root of these five objectives is *respect*. An obvious way to get what you want from people is to make them like and appreciate you. If they think highly of you, they will want to please you. They may even want to impress you.

An important part of this process involves an understanding of how and why challenging behaviour comes about in the classroom. This may require some personal reflection on your own practice, not always an easy thing to do. I hold the view that an incident of difficult behaviour has two sides: what the student brings to the situation, and what the teacher brings. While you cannot necessarily do much about what the student brings, you *can* control what you bring. You can approach a problem with integrity. In addition, you can endeavour to make sense of why a pupil may be acting/reacting in the way that they are. You can separate this from a 'Why do they always do this to me?' reaction. Be objective. Analyse challenging behaviour instead of falling victim to it, and learn to recognize how your actions and reactions can influence the outcome.

Build relationships with pupils

Positive student–staff rapport is perhaps one of the most valuable tools that any teacher can have. Without it, any kind of behaviour management intervention or system becomes much harder to achieve. The simple fact is, if a student likes and/or respects you they are going to be far more likely to want to please you, and thereby cooperate with you. If they dislike you, or sense that you dislike them, the opposite may unfold.

So, is it a popularity game? It doesn't have to be. From my experience, most students, particularly older ones, are suspicious of teachers who try too hard to be their 'mate'. They've got plenty of those already – they want teachers to have a 'human', personable side; but they still want them to be teachers, to be the ones who manage and guide and set standards. They expect teachers to be the nucleus of control within the classroom, and to challenge unacceptable behaviour. They may push the boundaries but, ultimately, they want those boundaries to contain them.

There are, of course, a million and one gimmicks to help get students on your side and many of them are very effective: chatting about the footy score/ *X Factor* result; having charisma; delivering 'fun' lessons; getting involved with broader school life (running clubs, plays, activity trips, etc.); offering bribes (sweets, stickers, privileges); smiling and greeting pupils as they come through the door, making them feel welcome.

But, fundamentally, that all-important rapport relies on creating the sense that your students and their learning *matters* to you; for example, that you take the trouble to thoughtfully mark their work, have enthusiasm for your subject, mean and do what you say you will, set high expectations and express encouragement and belief in them. In short, show them that you care.

4 | A thorough approach: how to get ahead of the challenge

In the following chapters, I will explore the key behavioural difficulties that challenging students may present to the classroom environment. In each chapter I will highlight the type of behaviour I am referring to and proceed with advice regarding measures that will prevent, act upon and follow-up the problem. The reason I place emphasis on prevention and follow-up is that if problematic behaviour in your classroom is to improve with lasting effect, there is a need to continuously promote and support positive ways of existing in the class environment. Make it a place where you and your pupils (including the tricky ones) would like to be.

There are no short cuts – but if you proactively seek to establish good order and responsible behaviour, and give as much support and credence to this as you would to other aspects of school life, you will see the results of your labours. You will feel like a master of your class environment. Your confidence will increase, your stress levels will decrease – the job might not become easier, but your ability to handle it will thrive. You might even find you enjoy it! Your behaviour management approach should take place on three levels.

Proactive

Do not wait for challenging behaviour to happen before you contemplate dealing with it – a few simple early interventions may mean you do not have to go that far. Better for you, and better for your students. This is not to say that you need to be the voice of doom, always expecting the worst from your charges (telling them off before they get caught). It is about being prepared – a teacher's mantra – anticipating difficulties, and being aware. Taking small steps at the early stages to prevent yourself from having to take big, difficult ones in times of stress. Knowing when, and how, to intervene is not an easy skill, but it can be a rewarding and interesting one to develop, requiring intuition, quick thinking and avid alertness.

Reactive

Things do not always go to plan, or they erupt from nowhere. Sometimes a situation can escalate so quickly that your preventative efforts get squashed in the stampede. Imagine you have just invited your class into the room. Immediately, two students begin arguing loudly between themselves. They are trying to settle a score that began during break. They are both volatile, and likely to resort to more 'physical' methods of communication. Not only this, but they are so fixated on their dispute, that they are oblivious to your requests to stop shouting. If you do not intervene straight away the situation may get out of hand. However, being taken by surprise (you've only just dismissed your previous class, and your thoughts are still somewhere with their unfinished coursework), and not knowing the origins of the argument, can leave you somewhat thrown.

Having an idea of what to do or what to say under pressure can give you an immense amount of reassurance and confidence. This aspect of behaviour management can seem the most intimidating – what to do when it all kicks off? Why do some teachers seem to know exactly how to tell a child off, yet others try it and get ignored or ridiculed? What is the secret? Actually, there is no secret. Managing a very challenging situation can, in some ways, be less demanding than trying to prevent one. Prevention requires creativity, intuition and energy. If you are already at the point of negotiating an enraged 10-year-old into leaving the classroom, your objective is set for you. There is just one thing to do: achieve it. The 'stuck record' approach – just repeating your request in a boring, flat voice until it is heeded – is simple, but surprisingly effective. The fact is, reactive methods of managing incidents of challenging behaviour tend to rely on repetition, simplicity and directness, rather than ingenuity. Know the formula, and then it is there for you when you need it.

Follow-up

The ability to prevent and, when necessary, deal directly with challenging behaviour is purely a panacea if 'follow-up' is not valued. By this, I refer to seeing through the consequences you may have set a student, discussing their behaviour with them, assisting them in resolving difficulties, establishing a resolution, monitoring and acknowledging improvements, and above all, encouraging them to take responsibility for their actions. In the hectic course of the day it is tempting to erase the memory of an unpleasant incident; but time invested in chasing up will improve the prospect of long-term classroom stability, showing you to be a reliable, strong and confident force to reckon with. Don't be the teacher that sends students out of the classroom for five minutes' time-out and then forgets they ever existed!

Yes. Yes. I know. It all seems like an awful lot of work, especially when there are a million and one other things to do. Why should organized teachers who enjoy their subject and give their life to the school and its students dedicate so much of the time they don't have to managing the ungrateful little sods who hate their lessons anyway? Tough. It's how things are. There are lots of questions to be asked and answered about teacher workload, stress and pressure. (Better still, there are lots of actual changes that could be made.) But for the purposes of this book, I am assuming we are all prepared to be forward-thinking. It is a matter, if necessary, of readjusting our priorities and refusing to bow to negative, defeatist attitudes surrounding our profession and its challenges. We can take the reins of our inclusive, mixed-ability, urban/rural/inner-city, multi-this, multi-that classrooms, and get the most out of the experience – for ourselves, and for our students.

As I've said before, there are no short cuts. If you have difficult students in your classes, and want to feel confident about managing them, want to see long-term improvement in attitude and attainment, want to feel like you have control of your job – be prepared to invest effort and energy. Do not expect progress to take place overnight as there are many factors working against you. But remember this, the more experience you have of managing challenging behaviour, the more confident you become – even if (especially if!) you have a few disasters along the way. If you are confident with challenging behaviour, there is going to be little else in the world that will faze you.

Dealing with details: tackling low-level disruption

With the term 'low-level disruption' I refer to those seemingly less-obtrusive behaviours that can slowly tap away at your nervous system. They are not the loud, obvious, lesson-stopping catastrophes that are frequently associated with challenging students – but they can be no less draining to deal with. They are the insidious and sneaky little details of the challenging behaviour showcase.

Relentless finger tapping. Fidgeting. Calling out. Arriving late. Making strange random noises. Swearing. Swinging on the back legs of the chair.

Though they are low-level in nature, they are often repetitive and extremely corrosive: eating away your patience and time. Imagine the chair-swinger (my personal nemesis). Despite all the stories about broken backs and nosebleeds, the constant reminders and the withdrawal of privileges – the swinger still goes for it. You want to ignore it – if they really want to swing that badly, let them. But visions of their spine shooting into their nasal cavity pester you into aggravation. Not to mention that niggling thought that if you let them get away with it, the whole class will have a go. Twenty-eight pupils clattering to the floor with their spines in their noses. Explain that to Ofsted!

One way or another, it is best to tackle the little details. It is your starting point. Getting the management of low-level disruption right will help you establish overall control in the classroom, and build a relationship of understanding between yourself and your students. The ESBD gospel implies that every tiny mishap is accounted for (for example, answering properly at the call of the register). Show them the limits early on, and they are less likely to push them.

Investing some time in smoothing out the small creases will pay long-term dividends. However, balance is the key. If your tone is perceived as too angry, too stroppy or too impatient, your efforts may be counter-productive. Students quickly lose affection for teachers whom they feel are unpredictable or irrational. From experience, I would surmise that *fairness* plays a very significant role in the minds of individuals with ESBD. If, in their view, you are being short-tempered or unreasonable, they may decide they are better off working against you. On the other hand, if you are too gentle in your approach it may be overlooked, marking you out to be an easy ride. A fine line: get the pitch right, and your life will be much easier. Get it wrong, and you may be making a rod for your own back. Aim to step down the middle: show them that you are sure of what you want, but that you are also a reasonable person.

The low-level disruptions I am going to focus on are the ones that I feel best represent students with particularly challenging behaviour, as opposed to the general 'naughty' activity that can occur in a classroom. The first of these is *fidgeting and restlessness*, the hallmarks of hyperactivity. The second is *attention-seeking* behaviour, which encompasses calling out, distracting other students and showing off.

The final focus is what I would describe as *attitude* behaviour – persistent casual late entrance to class, disinterest in the lesson, answering back.

These three areas are common stems of disruptive behaviour. Knowing how to make sense of, and work with, these challenges will provide grounding for dealing with difficulties of a more intrusive nature.

5 | Managing fidgeting and restlessness

Behaviour of this kind can be frustrating and time-consuming. A key concern is that the fidgety student is not concentrating, or is distracting others from concentrating. It can also be a burden on you if the behaviour is particularly persistent or repetitive. However, fidgeting and restlessness may be unintentional. Bear in mind that some students will have little control over their actions. For example, individuals with an attention deficit disorder will struggle to concentrate for long periods of time. They may find it difficult to sit still, or to keep their hands to themselves. In these circumstances your objective is not to eliminate the behaviour entirely, but to find ways of managing and working with it.

If not an attention deficit condition or hyperactivity, other causes of restlessness need to be considered. Is the student seeking attention from you or other students? Are they anxious? Are they coping with the work level/pace? Restless, distracted behaviour is often employed as a tactic to consciously (or sub-consciously) avoid getting down to task. If you can identify such a cause, you can work on the root of the problem.

Some proactive ideas are outlined below.

Reduce temptation

Have desktops as clear as possible when equipment and stationery is not being used. Until needed, request that stationery is not taken out of bags/pen-tidies, thus students are less likely to be distracted from listening and watching. Any equipment that has to remain on desks can be organized in a way that minimizes its accessibility. In the primary classroom (where tables may be grouped) use central pen-tidies, have exercise books/worksheets in piles or trays – elect a member of each table to be responsible for overseeing the tidiness, and do spot-checks!

Set up good habits

Encourage students to keep their desks tidy and put equipment away properly. For practical activities, have a structured approach to setting up/tidying, rather than a free-for-all (which carries ample opportunity for the ill treatment of equipment). Ensure that you incorporate adequate time for this to be achieved into your lesson structure.

Command 100 per cent attention

Always expect full attention from your students when you are addressing them. Consider how you want your students to show they are paying attention to you. Remind them to stop working, to put their pens/pencils down, to look up and listen. Allow a brief moment for them to follow this request. They may benefit from a cue: 'I would like everyone to look at me please . . . show me that you are listening.' Younger children can be encouraged to sit with arms folded, though older students may find this patronizing. Reminders about how students can show they are paying attention, backed up with praise for getting it right, will set helpful examples for the students that find it difficult.

Clutter free

The tidier your classroom is in general, the less stressful the space will be, not just for you, but for your students as well. Remember how refreshed and clear-minded you feel after having a big clear-out at home? The same effect can happen in the classroom. In an organized space, it is easier to see what is going on and where, making the task of keeping track of your students' behaviour more straightforward. Likewise, encouraging students to be tidy and organized (keeping their desks straight, remaining seated unless they've been given permission, lining up when requested to leave or enter a room) will foster responsible behaviour. It will also allow you to observe with clarity (and thus deal more swiftly with) any student who is pushing the boundaries.

Awareness

Know your students. If any of them are frequently distracted, restless or fidgety, find out why. Obtain and share information with your SENCO, and other staff who work with the student. Are difficulties known about? Have underlying causes been identified? Having this information will enable you to plan your strategies more effectively, as well as provide you with greater understanding of the problem. If you have understanding, it is easier to be tolerant.

Discuss the problem

Approach the student about the behaviour discreetly and with a non-confrontational tone. Be clear and open. Explain that you have become aware of the problem (e.g. they frequently get out of their seat and wander round the classroom when they should be working quietly). Check that they are aware of doing it – do they realize why it is not acceptable? Be understanding and positive, but firm in your wish that the behaviour should change. As has been discussed, some students will unintentionally find it difficult to control their behaviour. They may, themselves, be embarrassed and frustrated by it (I have seen this many times in the case of students with ADHD). Discuss ways in which you can help and work with them.

Encourage students to be self-aware

Include the student when developing effective strategies for dealing with their behaviour, encouraging them to take responsibility for their actions. For younger students, you could set up a small, personalized reward system/sticker chart to motivate them. For older (and younger) students, you could use a cue card, or agree on a special signal/hand gesture, that will discreetly remind them to sit still or re-focus without drawing too much attention to it. A friendly reminder that saves your voice! Another approach is to use an egg-timer or stopwatch to encourage a student to complete periods of focused concentration – time-limited so that it is less daunting and more measurable/rewarding. If these methods prove unsuccessful after a trial period, revisit the problem with the student – explore why it is not working, and then adapt the strategy. Perhaps a harder line needs to be taken – three reminders and then a consequence (e.g. move to a desk at the front of the class, time-out).

Some reactive ideas are outlined below.

Be calm

So you're near the end of an exhausting Tuesday. 8B: lively and fun when you've got the energy, utterly draining when you haven't. Billy's chair swinging is really irritating you (visions of the table sliding back, Billy crashing to the ground – the rest of the class laugh riotously, until they see the blood pouring from the gash in his head). What's more, you have told him a thousand times – is he deliberately trying to irritate you? . . . Take a deep breath. And have a *quiet* word in Billy's ear:

> 'You know that swinging on your chair is not acceptable – it's unsafe, and it's distracting – you need to sit up straight and focus on your work. Thank you.'

Speak as though you mean business, be explicit but focus on the behaviour – keep it direct and simple. Although you may be worn out and on the edge of your temper, angry authority (as opposed to calm authority) runs the risk of making a small situation bigger. We all resent anything that sounds like nagging, moaning or yelling, and ESBD students are particularly quick to react badly to this approach.

Move towards the problem

Physical presence is powerful, and useful when your voice is tired. If a student is being persistently distracted/distracting, move directly towards them, and gesture what you want. A hand signal to move their chair forward, put a pen down or stop nattering can be more effective than a verbal request. If you are talking to the rest of the class, carry on as you do this; it is not always necessary to disturb the flow of your lesson.

A caution: think carefully before trying to take an item from a student in a bid to stop them fiddling with it, particularly if the item is personal to the student. Such situations can often trigger conflict, with the item becoming a tool of control-seeking behaviour. Never, ever try to snatch an item – it is clumsy, intrusive and more often than not, ineffective. Move towards the student calmly, request that they hand the item to you with a commanding but polite voice, but give an alternative – you may suggest that they put it away or place it on your desk – thus they do not have to submit directly to you.

Assure them that if you see them playing with the offending item again, then it will have to be confiscated until the end of the day.

Use the sliding scale of intervention

A key aspect of managing challenging behaviour is to be measured and calm in your response, and to create opportunities for the student to put things right. Emphasize good choices that are made, and ensure that any consequences set are reasonable. This is particularly important when dealing with low-level disruptions, for if these situations are seen to escalate out of reasonable control – you scream at a volatile student whose persistent pen tapping is wearing you down, he or she calls you a 'f**king c**t'. Two quiet, but firm, warnings with reference to the potential consequence of the behaviour, and then, if necessary, followed up with the enactment of the consequence itself, gives the student the responsibility of deciding their fate:

'Andrea. You need to look this way please.'

She initially takes notice, but after a minute she is chatting to the people sitting behind her again.

'Andrea. This is your second warning. You need to turn around and concentrate on your work, or you will have to move to another table. Make the right choice.'

Again, she fails to heed your advice.

'Andrea –'
'Aw. Miss. I don't wanna move . . . '
'I'm sorry, but you've made that choice for yourself. Next time think more carefully about what you want to happen. Come and sit here with no more fuss, and that will be the end of the matter . . . Thank you.'

If you familiarize yourself with this pattern of verbal intervention, and have a prior idea of the sort of consequences that would befit such behaviour, seeing it through can be very straightforward and less stress-inducing than shouting.

Work with the behaviour

In some instances, getting control of fidgety behaviour may be too difficult for the student to achieve. Is there any way that you can tolerate this behaviour without it distracting you or the class? For example, the student with 'busy' hands may be given a piece of felt or cloth to satisfy the habit – pleasingly silent! For some students, being able to keep their hands busy may aid their concentration rather than hinder it.

Some follow-up ideas are outlined below.

Reward improvements

Praise students who have made an effort to contain their own behaviour, or have quickly responded to reminders. It may be appropriate to include these students in class awards or certificates. Bear in mind, something that may have felt like a mere irritation to you could have been remarkably difficult for the student to overcome. Make them feel that not doing it is worth the effort.

Monitor progress

It is useful to keep an eye on students who have, or have had, restless behaviours, as change or recurrence of these problems can be an early indication that something is up. They may increase at times of anxiety, or may reflect that the student is struggling to keep up with the work level. If the student is on medication, is it being taken correctly? Is the dosage appropriate?

Share information

It is important that knowledge is spread among the individuals who are connected with the student in question. If you have found a strategy that works well, inform other teachers – consistency is one of the most powerful factors in successfully managing challenging students. Perhaps parents have useful insight into the problem: dietary issues, poor sleeping habits. Likewise, they may be grateful for any advice or thoughts you can share with them.

6 | Managing attention-seeking behaviour

Recognizing attention-seeking behaviour is not hard – look in any household, workplace or classroom. We all do it to varying degrees: we all want affirmation that we are cared about, that our existence is worthwhile. For young people with emotional and behavioural issues, this can be taken to extremes.

The origins and causes of attention-seeking behaviour are complex, wide-ranging and personalized, but I would suggest lack of self-esteem has a significant role. The behaviour may be transient, corresponding to temporary circumstances or difficulties in a student's life, or it may be a well-established, ingrained way of existing. Examples of this behaviour can range from neediness (the child who constantly looks to you for reassurance and who struggles to function independently) to boisterous, antagonistic bursts of disruption.

For many students it is a coping mechanism: a misguided way of fulfilling the need to feel valid. An individual with a compulsion to seek excessive attention from others is unlikely to be a very secure person. Next time you feel the annoyance rise in your throat, as Stacey from 9F puts her feet up on her desk and starts shrieking about how great her new shoes are, remind yourself that she is probably trying to make up for a true lack of self-worth.

A substantial amount of challenging classroom behaviour can be classified as seeking attention in inappropriate ways. Attention is a confused goal for so many young people, who may be hindered by emotional immaturity, undeveloped social skills, and lack of awareness of themselves and others. As a teacher, you may not see your role as the nurturing and unravelling of a vulnerable mind, but if you can develop a holistic way of managing this issue, you may have a significant effect on the individual's emotional development, as well as maintaining acceptable behaviour in your lessons.

The management of attention-seeking behaviour has several aims: to boost self-esteem, to encourage independence and to reframe ways of seeking and obtaining attention (shifting from negatives to positives).

Some proactive ideas are outlined below.

Know your students

Find out what you can from the SENCO, head of year, tutor or parents about what is going on for these students. Many would suggest that attention-seeking behaviour is actually attention-*needing*, brought about by unfulfilled emotional and/or physical requirements. For example, children who have experienced abuse or neglect; children who have low self-esteem; children who are having difficulties with socialization, or have experienced loss or trauma. Sensitivity to these factors, will help you to separate your feelings about the behaviour (probably negative!) from your compassion for the student.

Set up good habits

Students seeking attention may be prone to calling out at inappropriate times. If all students are encouraged to put up their hands in order to speak aloud, there is a clear model of behaviour that they can be redirected to. By having some set procedures in place (for example, remaining seated and putting up your hand when you have finished working; lining up; remaining silent while the register is taken) you will create a structured environment in which inappropriate attention-seeking behaviour will stand out. There will be a benchmark in place to show the acceptable alternative. This may sound obvious, but I have observed a number of lessons missing such structured procedures, and found that the really challenging students were able to camouflage their disruptive behaviour against a backdrop of general chaos, making it difficult to monitor.

Be 'inclusive'

Make a conscious effort to include students with behavioural problems into the lesson. Give them attention for the right reasons. It is all too easy for students to become sidelined if they have missed substantial amounts of schooling through poor attendance or exclusions. Of course, the scenario for you is far from ideal – the rest of the class are moving on and naturally you want to focus on them, what can you do for the child that rarely attends? But making a small effort to show that you value a student's presence in the classroom could have a significant effect on their self-esteem. I once supported an

ESBD Year 8 boy who was starting to attend mainstream school for one day a week. With a history of exclusions and poor academic levels to match, he was a fish out of water in a fast-paced ICT session. Trying his best to impress, he would constantly raise his hand with the other students to answer questions. Knowing he did not have a hope of getting an answer right, his teacher would, however, give him an opportunity to answer out loud every week and always praised his contributions. ICT, he pronounced to me later, was his very best lesson.

Some reactive ideas are outlined below.

To ignore or not to ignore?

I am yet to be convinced that ignoring behaviour is truly productive in the classroom environment. It has often been advocated as a way of avoiding fulfilling a child's inappropriate demands for attention. In theory, the child should get bored of their unsuccessful protest and give up. In truth, I have frequently seen this approach have the opposite effect for ESBD students. Instead of getting bored and settling back down, they go to the next level – such is the intensity of their drive to be noticed. What starts as a small bit of wriggling about during carpet time becomes crawling under the tables pretending to be a caged animal! If the goal of any inappropriate behaviour is attention, failing to receive this attention may lead to more extreme bids for the desired result. Not only this, but ignoring behaviour can put yourself and the rest of the class under duress – attention-seeking behaviour is designed to be distracting. Trying not to be distracted can be very hard work indeed. However, there are times when a bit of *tactical* ignorance can be very effective. Using this method in conjunction with considered comments can be a helpful low-level intervention:

> 'That doesn't interest me, Jamie . . . I'm going over to speak to these students, because they are listening well. If you decide to listen too, then you can be part of the group – and that will be nice!'

Reframing

By reframing, I mean encouraging and redirecting students towards acceptable ways of achieving their goals, in this instance: attention.

If a student persistently calls out during class discussion, instead of replying to their comment or telling them off, calmly remind them of the need to put up their hand before commenting. When they get it right, respond and praise them for the behaviour – show them positive attention for positive reasons.

Avoid reinforcing negative efforts to gain attention by not over-reacting to these. Even adverse reactions can satisfy the attention-needy: *any* interest is better than none. Simply redirect the student to a more appropriate method, and reinforce this with praise and positive attention. It need not be complicated:

> 'Lucy, you need to stop calling out. I will very happily come and look at what you are doing when I can see that you are sitting back down and concentrating on your task.'

Model desired behaviour

It is not always enough just to tell a child what you want them to do and expect them to comply. For younger students, or those who have long been allowed to get attention for inappropriate reasons, alternatives may be unfamiliar to them. No matter how many times you calmly remind a student to raise their hand and stay seated when their work is completed, the old habit of getting up and clambering over to you, waving their half-finished worksheet (and interfering with other students along the way), still recurs. Some individuals need to see to believe. Time invested in sitting with a student, talking through and *demonstrating* how you want them to behave will help drive the message home. Assure the individual that you will be pleased if they do this. Model behaviour in the way you would model a science experiment or the construction of an essay: visual examples, clear guidelines, checking their understanding.

Focus on others

Divert your attention to the ones who are getting it right. Emphasize that you are pleased with them, and explain why:

> 'Jimmy. Sarah. I can see that you are listening and ready to start the lesson. Well done.'

This reinforces the idea that teacher attention will be given to those behaving appropriately.

'I am waiting for others to do the same.'

This provides a further hint, without drawing negative attention specifically to the perpetrator(s).

Be explicit

Think of the student who cannot seem to leave other classmates alone. Always pulling at their clothes, snatching their things, poking them in the back, pushing and barging them in the line-up: the individual that does not know how to make meaningful connections with others, and resorts to crude, physical grabs for attention. This misguided provocative behaviour only serves to alienate the individual further, as other students become wary of interacting with them.

If you witness this sort of behaviour, address it and clearly explain why it is inappropriate ('It disturbs/hurts/annoys others'). Inform the student that it will not be tolerated and elicit an apology, but do not go down the route of: 'No one will like you if you hit/scratch/poke them!' Of course, this is true – but glib phrases like this can corrode a child's self-esteem. If you wish to see long-term improvement, ensure that you work *with* the students' problems and promote successful ways of gaining attention, rather than simply dismissing the unsuccessful ones. Imply that you understand what they are trying to do, but that you have some ideas about how they could do it more effectively:

> 'Karina gets upset when you pull her hair, because it hurts her. If you would like her to play a game with you, you need to show her that you are not going to hurt her, and that you can have fun together. How could you do this?'
> 'Talking?'
> 'Yes. Good idea – ask her if she will play with you. Shall we try it out?'

A perfect opportunity to model and role-play the new technique. A telling-off may deter a child, but it will not teach them new skills.

Some follow-up ideas are outlined below.

Work with the others

If an individual repeatedly harasses other students for attention, it is important to reassure and advise the targeted students why they are being treated in this way, thus reducing the risk of an unpleasant backlash. A meeting with these students to consider why the particular young person may be behaving the way he or she is – allowing thoughts to be aired and developing ways of understanding and improving the situation – may prove valuable in terms of supporting relationships between class members. Give these students some non-confrontational strategies for responding to the behaviour (move away/ask them to stop/speak to an adult) and encourage them to adopt a helpful approach to including that person. Peers can be remarkably mature and supportive of one another given a little direction. If you have such networks as peer mentoring or 'buddies' in your school, these will be useful.

Acknowledge improvements

Give as much positive support, encouragement and attention as you can – for the right reasons – and your students will be less likely to seek it in other ways. If a student has made progress with their behaviour, remark on this – if they have made lots of progress, make a special point of it (for example, speak to their tutor or senior staff, perhaps a phone-call home). If they slip back, remind them of the times that they did well; remind them of their capabilities. Remember, an attention-needy ESBD student may be lacking in self-esteem (hence the need to constantly reassure themselves that they are noticeable). If you can help build their confidence, and restore it if it wanes, you can bring about long-term change.

Provide specific attention time

I was once asked to observe a young girl who was plaguing her teacher with unwelcome demands for attention. Knowing something of the child's background, I was aware of distressing circumstances facing her and her family at that time. It was clear that she was desperate for reassurance and affection, but unskilled in demonstrating this – and having no one else, her teacher bore the brunt of this need. She had poor social skills and lacked friends. The teacher agreed to offer five minutes daily, during morning break, to give the girl some focused time – he would ask how she was, chat, have her help him tidy up, play a game – whatever he did, he was making her feel welcome and valued, and developing a trusting relationship. He incorporated some reliable classmates into the sessions, who eventually took over the role. Though she remained a troubled individual, her inappropriate bids for attention were significantly reduced. Sometimes students need extra support and comfort. Maybe you can suitably provide that, or know of others who can.

Share information

The need for attention can reflect vulnerability, low self-esteem, or difficult circumstances at home, which may need to be addressed. If you have reason to be concerned so might others, or perhaps they can shed light on the reasons behind the behaviour. If strategies and approaches to dealing with an individual's problem can be shared and consistently applied – with all staff drawing the same line between what is acceptable and what is not – the lesson on 'how to get people to notice you for the right reasons' will be much clearer.

7 | Managing attitude

Sometimes it feels like the efforts you make to carefully guide and educate your students are being undermined by the sweeping undercurrent of the cocky 'I'm my own master' attitude. How can you convince Sam that he is better off paying attention and following your instructions, when everything about him states that he doesn't give a monkey's? You remind him of the importance of arriving on time: 'Yeah yeah. Sorry. Whatever.' You request that he removes his earphones during the lesson: 'Ah Miss . . . chill out. Music makes me work better.' You insist that he stops chatting and starts working: (grunts) 'Yeah whatever – you're always moaning, man . . . you need to chill out.' It is painful to witness this lack of foresight – no sense of the value of education. It is frustrating, and often insulting, to be on the receiving end of such arrogant defiance of respectful communication. But the most disappointing thing of all is the sense that you'll never be able to get through to this particular individual. He will always seek to undermine you, and defy your requests, for the sake of . . . defying your requests. Attitude, man!

But that is all it is. A veneer of confidence and power. In modern society, it is as though attitude has replaced body armour in terms of providing self-protection. Promoting an attitude of self-importance, flippancy, or sometimes aggression, can keep others away from your vulnerable bits: weakness is not celebrated. Remind yourself that behind all the challenging, irritating, cocky, arrogant behaviour – there is an insecure, mousy individual trying to make it in the big, bad world.

For young people with complex emotional issues, demonstrating that they are in control of a situation (as opposed to the teacher being in control of them) can be more than just a bit of attitude, it can be an instinct of survival – a way of keeping safe and powerful. Imagine how important this is to the individual who has had traumatic experiences of disempowerment in their young life: abuse, inconsistent parenting, bullying or neglect. An excellent reason to avoid confrontational/power-seeking approaches to telling off: do this to a child who fears control being taken from them, and you can be sure that they will fight to keep control. Yell at them, and they will yell back louder. Intimidate them, and they will try to intimidate you more. A negative situation escalating out of control . . . but who's to blame?

Some proactive ideas are outlined below.

Promote respect

If you actively encourage students to relate to you and each other in positive ways, and make this part of your classroom expectations, you are setting up an environment that provides plenty of exemplary behaviour.

◆ Have 'respect each other' as one of your class rights/rules.
◆ Use PSHCE/tutorial sessions as an opportunity to explore the issue and its importance. Explore what respect means to different people.
◆ Encourage students to reflect on their own behaviour and attitudes to one another.
◆ Use case studies and role-play to consider the cause and effect of respect/disrespect.

Identify weaknesses and motivations

If a student has an attitude of reluctance and disengagement with the classroom, make an effort to get to know them. Surprise them by showing a non-confrontational interest in what they like/dislike about school. The mere fact that they are being listened to, that their views are being acknowledged, may help them relate more positively to the classroom experience you provide. Through building a relationship with a student, you may come closer to understanding what makes them tick (i.e. cut through the armour of attitude), and you can use this to motivate them. For example, Kevin's ambition is to release a rap album . . . what skills do rap artists need? Literacy, surely? Numeracy, to know when they've reached Number One. Business studies, to outwit those greedy accountants. Languages might be useful – all that exciting foreign travel. But Kevin also thinks that school is a waste of time, and he hates people telling him what to do.

'Kevin, don't sell yourself short. Use the opportunities around you to help you get what you want. If you don't want people having a go at you, make the choice not to do the things that wind them up. Show them that you don't need to be nagged, because you can take good responsibility for yourself . . .'

Okay. So a few common-sense pearls of wisdom will not reform Kevin overnight, but with persistence, it might be his starting point for developing some self-belief.

Feel prepared

Know what your response to cocky attitude will be, for it is one of those things that can be very disarming when you are not expecting it, especially given the natural instinct to want to preserve your own dignity and strength in front of the rest of the class. If you have a pre-conceived notion of what you consider to be acceptable/unacceptable levels of respectfulness – and a few stock responses in mind – you are better equipped to deal with the behaviour in an efficient, clean manner.

Some reactive ideas are outlined below.

Remain neutral

Though you may feel compelled to tear strips off the cheeky little so-and-so (as he bluntly informs you that *you're* the one with the problem, not him), bear in mind that reacting with anger is playing his game. You ask him to follow an instruction. He tries to take control, by belittling you. You try to take it back, by showing him who's boss ('Don't you dare speak to me like that!'). Whether the power struggle progresses further or not, no one has learned anything about how to communicate effectively. It is a doomed situation. However, if you go against internal instincts, and deflate the student's comment by remaining personally ambivalent, you will avoid courting the power trap. You can show your disapproval without getting emotional:

'That's inappropriate – we need to remember to speak respectfully to one another in our classroom.'

Mel goes a step further and mimics you rudely:

> '"That's inappropriate" . . . blah blah blah.'
> 'And that, too, is inappropriate, Mel. If you wish, we can discuss this issue after school – but if you don't want that to happen, then I suggest you show me your more charming side!'

For the student, it will be hard to rise to such a diffusive reaction without looking slightly silly. (And you always have the staffroom to go to and vent your anger!)

Turn negatives into positives

If a student is being cheeky or antagonistic, they are perhaps struggling to cope with the rigours and expectations of the learning environment. Attitude often masks feelings of inadequacy or insecurity. Students may attempt to avoid the pressure of classroom success (or fear of failure) by creating diversions: pretending they are not bothered, belittling the experience. They can quickly be disarmed if you show passive disinterest in this kind of behaviour, and, instead, focus on drawing them into the lesson, encouraging their contributions. A sense of humour is useful here:

> 'Alex, I can see that you've got a lot to say for yourself today . . . what do *you* think about Chapter Six?'
> 'It's a load of crap . . .' (He grins and looks to the rest of the class for support).
> 'So you're trying to tell me you think it's no good . . . can you explain that further using more helpful language? It's no good because . . . ?'
> 'I dunno . . .'
> 'Well, I'd be interested to hear your opinion. Why don't you think about your answer and then I'll come back to you later. In the meantime, does anyone else agree with Alex?'

Defer your response

If the attitude is persistent or particularly obtuse, make it clear to the student that there will be a further consequence for the behaviour. In the heat of the moment, it is easy to make menacing threats (detention for a week!) in order to express the frustration and anger you feel, and to ensure that your point has been made more clearly than theirs. But, are you *really* prepared to chase up this kind of consequence? The time and effort it involves: perhaps holding detention yourself, setting work, following up with staff to ensure the detention is attended (for a week), chasing up the student if they do not attend.

And as the frustrations of the moment subside – returning to your usual state of peace and tranquillity – did the behaviour really justify such a weighty sanction? You need to rationalize how grave an incident is, and then set a consequence that reflects this. If it is difficult to do this in a measured way at that particular moment, defer your response: tell the student they will need to see you after the lesson. (If you are prone to forgetfulness, write a reminding note for yourself.)

You now have time to calm down; to think of an appropriate consequence; to give the student opportunity to redeem him or herself; and to focus on the rest of the lesson. When it comes to it, retaining a student at the end of the lesson may be consequence enough (especially if it is break / lunch / end of the day), accompanied by a firm conversation about respect. If not, then address the behaviour, emphasize cause and effect, set the consequence and remind the student that the next lesson will be an opportunity to start afresh. Be firm, direct and measured.

Some follow-up ideas are outlined below.

See things through

Any effort to address behaviour through setting consequences needs to be reliable. As has been discussed, the consequence should fit the crime, and it should then be carried out as swiftly as possible. Stay true to whatever you say you will do, otherwise you risk losing the 'fear factor' with your students. (This applies to every aspect of your behaviour management, not just dealing with bad attitude.) Don't make threats unless you are confident that you will be able to enact them if necessary. If you make a threat, the student may well rise to it – be true to your word, or they will start to see that they can manipulate you.

Students who come to school with the 'I can do as I please' attitude may not be intimidated by warnings of potential sanctions. They are likely to be the kind of students who will fail to turn up for detention, or defy requests for sorry letters or homework. In this instance, it is helpful if you can work with your colleagues. They can support you in following things through (for instance, escorting the student to your room, helping to chase things up, giving reminders). It is important not to let things go – if they fail to comply with the original consequence, what is in place for this? Be warned: if a student is determined, they can avoid consequence after consequence – turning the situation into one of ridicule. What then? Request the support of senior staff, who can take the matter into their hands, but make sure you are kept in the loop.

Show that you are interested

Setting consequences/sanctions for rude or lazy attitudes may reinforce the fact that this is not acceptable in the classroom: but this approach might have little effect on the recurrence of such behaviour. This is because the cause and effect principle (behave like this, then this consequence will follow) does not necessarily impact on the origins of the problem. Attitude is the result of many factors in a person's life: whether they are encouraged to learn and follow rules, whether life seems fair, whether they are taught to trust people or to stand up to them. These preconceptions cannot be quickly or easily changed, but my experience has shown me that students are more likely to make progress in this area if they feel that you actually care about them. Make your students feel that you specifically want them to be part of your class (as opposed to just another pupil passing through the doors).

In a busy mainstream setting, it is simply not possible to give every student the due care and attention you may (or may not!) wish to, especially the intense levels often required by students with emotional and behavioural difficulties. But it is not too much effort to ensure that you promote positivity in your classroom. Provide praise and encouragement when challenging students try, or get it right. Remind them that they are valued in the classroom, even though their behaviour is sometimes not. When resolving difficulties, end conversations on a positive note. Show the student that you are the kind of person that they should want to please, because pleasing you is worth the effort – you are fair, you are kind, you are supportive (not to mention fun, dynamic, wacky, good-looking, interesting, semi-famous . . .).

Engage the parents/guardians

So it can be hard work getting through to a student who just does not seem to care. How can you deter an individual from behaving in a certain way, if their attitude implies that they are not bothered? As I have previously discussed, one powerful tool in your armour is knowing an individual's motivations and weaknesses. Manipulative perhaps, but there is productive value to be gained from using an individual's weaknesses against them – parents/guardians can be useful in this respect. Some of the disruptive, disengaged students I have worked with were more responsive to the intervention or involvement of their parents/guardians above everything else. Building up a dialogue between yourself and these people can be an effective way of policing behaviour – a phone-call home to inform them of a disappointing lesson's events can be more powerful than a year's worth of detention. A phone-call home to relay good news about pleasing improvements in attitude and behaviour can be just as powerful for the opposite reason. (In the age of computer technology, regular, convenient contact via email might not be out of place.) All of this, of course, depends on whether the student has an effective, safe relationship with their parents/guardians. Sadly, this is not always the case.

A recurring problem when dealing with the parents of students with challenging behaviour is that the parents themselves may have needs or problematic behaviours – it is the cyclical nature of ESBD, issues are often passed down the generations. Trying to engage their support and interest can be a challenge in itself. In this situation, a collaborative effort is most effective, with professionals from different backgrounds – for example, education, social services, health and psychology – working together to provide coordinated support for vulnerable individuals and their families. If you have concerns about a child's home-life or relationship with their parents/guardians, or are perhaps struggling to get any input from them, seek advice and information from your SENCO or Child Protection Officer (CPO).

Gifted and talented . . . but lazy

How do we motivate pupils who aren't necessarily lacking in ability, but lacking in application? A comment I often hear from teachers is: 'It's not my lower set groups that are the trouble . . . it's my top sets. They're lazy and arrogant and act like they already know it all.'

Faced with a class or student of this ilk, the first thing I would ask myself is where is this attitude coming from?

Unfortunately, the ingredients of intellect and youth don't automatically combine to make well-adjusted individuals. They are still susceptible to self-esteem issues, anger, insecurity and resentment. Quite often, lack of motivation is intentional – a protest against those who seem to 'want' or expect something from them: parents/teachers/society/themselves. In this way, we can see arrogance and laziness as just another of those veneers, a means of deflecting attention away from the real pressure. The challenge is finding a means of breaking through that veneer, and enabling students to see the value of their education . . . and the value of themselves as learners.

Start by looking for signs of boredom. How hard is your teaching working? Unless their minds are stretched, able students can be quick to disengage. And if it isn't lack of challenge, could it be subject-related? Find out how these students get on in other lessons – for example, their diligent approach to Maths may be completely different to their attitude in Art – which doesn't make it easy if you're their Art teacher, but knowing this at least gives you some leverage:

> 'Alex, I've been talking to Mr Green. He informs me that he's keen to enter you into the Maths challenge this year . . . but he's looking for students who are all-rounders. He's asked me to give him feedback on your effort in creative subjects, so hopefully this term you'll give me lots of reasons to say good things!'

Stepping up a level: dealing with medium-level disruption

Having considered a range of strategies to help you contain low-level disruptions, I wish to reflect on what to do when behaviour goes a step further. There will be times when a student's determination to 'express themselves' will override your determination to stop them. In the following sections I will explore ideas for addressing this kind of behaviour; though if you have managed to get a good grip on managing general low-level behaviour, such occurrences should be infrequent.

More serious incidents of challenging behaviour are often owned by just a few individuals within a class: the 'troublemakers'. These are the students who struggle to comprehend and conform to boundaries, may perform badly with their work, have difficulties remaining 'on-task' and seem to delight in rubbing you up the wrong way.

The issues I will be focusing on are *general disruption* and *uncooperative behaviour*: the student who will go to any length to distract and show-off in front of the class, and then blatantly refuse to follow your requests to comply with appropriate behaviour.

8 | Dealing with group disruption

Without doubt, facing a class that feels more like a mob is one of the biggest behaviour management nightmares going. No matter where you are at in your teaching career – newly qualified or old hand – the prospect is always a daunting one. One, or even two, challenging students can usually be addressed with minimum drain on your sensibilities, but if there is a larger group and they are all playing off each other, it can be hard to know where to even start.

Either they don't get on and constantly wind each other up – distracted from work by petty arguments and slanging matches across the classroom – or they get on too well, and get a rise out of winding *you* up! There is nothing more frustrating than falling victim to deliberate lesson sabotage: coordinated, premeditated behaviour designed to irritate: humming, whistling or tapping. The pack mentality can be a very powerful and intimidating force. Safety in numbers.

And sometimes there is no malicious coordination involved – it's just the mix of students, all too needy and chaotic to be able to get themselves focused and settled. Constant wandering, constant calling out, constant mucking around . . . and if you divert your attention towards the students in one corner of the room, the other corner starts up. In this instance, teaching becomes more like fire-fighting: continuously having to dampen down the little sparks before they escalate into raging pyres.

Add to this the pressure of addressing the needs of that handful of students who *are* there to work: some who might meekly plough on, but who nevertheless deserve better; and others who, when they have adequate teacher support, are able to get their heads down, but are just as likely to get sucked into the silliness if that teacher attention isn't forthcoming.

The problem is a complicated one, so naturally there is no simple solution. However, this section aims to provide some light at the end of the tunnel. There is no magic wand, but these tried and tested approaches should at least make the process easier.

Some proactive ideas are outlined below.

Seek support

Sometimes an extra pair of eyes and ears can help you identify flash-points and problem areas which you may otherwise miss because your own attention is too stretched. Ask a trusted colleague to spend some 'detective' time in a difficult lesson, subtly watching how the dynamics unfold. Their feedback may shed light on the origins of the problem and who the ringleaders are.

Alternatively, you may want to recruit the influence of a senior member of staff, or someone with a reputation for strong discipline, who can 'appear' in your classroom at a strategic time and use their sway to establish respectful calm. This is not to take away or detract from your role as leader within the classroom, but to demonstrate solidarity among a staff team and to give you the breathing space to make your own inroads with regards to self-assertion and pupil–teacher relations.

A lot of teachers, including the new and the experienced, have found this to be extremely helpful. Many say that a few initial 'visits' from SMT are required – sometimes it is enough for them to be walking past the classroom or lingering in the corridor – and beyond that, the teacher is able to reclaim authority. The students know that the school 'heavies' are only a whistle away and fully support what the teacher is doing.

The simple fact is, when up against a 'pack' of students, it takes a considerably strong individual personality to break through to them. If they're working as a team, then why shouldn't you? Asking for support is by no means about admitting your own defeat, but rather about maximizing available resources. Staff should support each other in this way – we all have strengths in different areas and the more we can pull those together, the more we can gain and learn from one another.

Change one thing

With extremely difficult groups, trying to change too much at once will wear you out, and may even make things worse, causing distraction, stress and confusion. Set yourself a realistic goal of aiming to establish one key rule or expectation amongst the students, and then build up from there. If students get into the *habit* of complying with one expectation, a pattern will be set and adding further expectations will be easier.

A simple rule to start with could be 'Enter the classroom quietly' or 'Listen while the teacher is talking'. Just work and work and work on that, even if it takes the majority of the lesson, or perhaps a number of lessons. If students protest, then explain to them that until they can manage this basic requirement, you can't imagine how you'll be able to teach them more exciting lessons. Remind them that the responsibility is theirs and that they need to demonstrate the capacity to co-operate with you in order for things to progress.

This approach works with both younger and older students. The beauty of it is that, as soon as you start seeing progress, you can create opportunities for positive reinforcement – lots of praise and encouragement for the fact that they are now trying to work 'with' you. This encouragement will hopefully have an impact on their self-esteem (which is often one of the root causes of badly performing groups – they know they are regarded as the class from hell, so they might as well live up to it). If their esteem is raised, their motivation to improve will increase and your relationship with them may take a U-turn. Certainly, some of the worst-behaved groups have ended up being my favourites. Step by step is the way forward.

Make an entrance

It is possible to increase your chances of having an impact on a rowdy class by using force of personality. Assertiveness is a powerful tool – if students sense that you are not intimidated or unsettled by their activities, they are more likely to take direction from you. After all, they *want* clear leadership even if they act like they don't.

Projecting a confident, assertive message of leadership isn't about shouting or throwing your weight around (an easy way to get caught up in power struggles). In fact, some of the most effective teachers can be extremely quiet. They make their presence felt through being calmly controlled and unflinchingly consistent.

If an authoritative presence doesn't come naturally (and, rest assured, for many people it doesn't) then it is important to 'adopt' that mental state before the lesson begins. Briefly think yourself into the idea that YOU are the commander; that YOU are the one who makes decisions and has the final say; the students are there to LEARN from YOU.

I've seen far too many teachers throw away the start of their lessons, entering the room or greeting students in an uncertain, disorganized manner. Even if you don't feel organized or self-assured, fake it! It's so important to set the right tone from the beginning. And having too many things to do (e.g. preparing resources, clearing up after the previous group, taking the register, dealing with homework) should not be an excuse. With difficult groups, your priority needs to be getting them settled under your wing. Of course, transition from lesson to lesson can be a busy time, but it's nothing that a bit of advanced preparation cannot solve. It also helps to establish a routine:

◆ How students enter the room/where they sit. Lining up outside the classroom? Standing behind desks? Seating plans?
◆ Time for you to greet students/identify and address any issues or attitudes that they have brought in with them – a simple starter activity for the rest of the class to be getting on with (something straightforward that doesn't require your explanation, e.g. anagram or puzzle).
◆ How/when/where they sort out their bags, coats and equipment.
◆ How the register is taken – formally, requiring all students to group together and pay attention, or discreetly, once the lesson has been established?

Some reactive ideas are outlined below.

How to get whole-class attention

Throughout the years, I have come across many tricks and gimmicks to aid this challenge (writing names on whiteboard, using timers, everyone putting their hands on their heads, looking at your watch and pretending to be bored), but, fundamentally, getting students to focus on you when you want them to relies on the aforementioned – projecting an assertive message of leadership. Getting student attention is so much easier if they respect your leadership and feel that something is at stake, e.g. they may miss something interesting, funny or important, or there may be consequences. Observe a confident personality (perhaps another teacher, public speaker or TV presenter) . . . what is it they do that makes them impossible to ignore?

Voice and body language make a difference – speak slowly and lower your pitch. Use volume and tone strategically, raising it to get attention, and softening to explain or create lighter moments. Stand with shoulders relaxed, arms open, palms out and use your position – move around the classroom so that your presence can be felt in all corners. Use physical position and eye contact to direct your teaching towards students who aren't paying attention.

For difficult groups, make sure there are clear and familiar consequences for individuals not paying attention. A series of warnings and a sliding scale of consequences can be effective. For example:

1st/2nd warnings – teacher makes a verbal/written note.
3rd warning – see teacher after break/school.
4th warning – 20-minute detention.
5th warning – removal from class/phone-call home.

A system such as this may not entirely eliminate interruptions, but if you stick with it, it will influence the majority of the class who will see that you're not going give up on raising expectations. Be sure to praise and possibly reward students who are doing the right thing – but consider doing this discreetly. Among hardened groups, students may feel uncomfortable about public praise, for fear of being picked on.

How to sustain whole-class attention

When you get attention, don't waste it. Be prepared with what to say and seize the opportunity. Give clear, direct instructions. Avoid too many words and hesitations, and try not to add '. . . okay?' on the end. Don't imply that there is a choice when there isn't one. Rather than repeat yourself, ask a student to repeat instructions back to you. If you pick a different student each time, they'll all be on tenterhooks in case it's their turn.

Alternatively, you may wish to jump in with a topic introduction. Whether this involves a demonstration, explanation or discussion, make sure you project enthusiasm. If the introduction involves a monologue from you, put colour into your voice (variations of volume and tone) and be careful not to 'over' talk. If you don't want student attention to wane, avoid unrealistic expectations – some classes can barely cope with a few minutes of listening to teacher. Keep it short, sharp and preferably entertaining. Break up chunks of lengthy explanation with question and answer sessions or tasks that involve different skills.

If at any point during your exposition you receive unwelcome interruptions (we've all had a taste of that 'just got them quiet . . . then someone pipes up again . . . and it's back to square one' experience), don't fluster or lose your cool. Stay neutral and have a plan –

if you have established a sliding scale of warnings/consequences, such as the one described previously, you can use this against disruptive individuals. Also, refer to the rules:

> 'I'll remind you that in this class, I have the right to teach and you have the right to learn. That means we need to listen. As you know, there'll be consequences for anyone who tries to interrupt or stop others from listening.'

Some follow-up ideas are outlined below.

Restoring order after a difficulty

Significant incidents of problem behaviour, even if they only involve one or two students, can easily affect the mood of the whole classroom. The teacher may sense an increase in excitability or reduced concentration, and if the class have had to witness any aggressive or threatening behaviour there may be a tense, anxious or shocked atmosphere within the room. None of these are conducive to productive learning and the lesson itself may need to be adapted.

This is where *flexibility* becomes an invaluable teaching skill. Judge the mood of the group before attempting to plough on with your lesson plan. If they are 'hyper' then it may pay to incorporate a calm settling activity, such as group reading or 'heads down' individual work – a folder of stand-by worksheets/activity ideas can be useful in this situation. Anything that involves lots of movement or free discussion, or is particularly challenging and rigorous, will be too demanding at this point. I have witnessed too many teachers wear themselves out by trying to continue with complex lesson activities, when what is really needed is a chance for them and the students to have a breather before getting on with things.

This principle can also be used as an incentive for motivating difficult groups in general. If they fail to cope with the more exciting, adventurous activities you offer them (i.e. they ignore instructions, get silly in discussions, or misuse equipment), bring them back down to earth with more formal tasks. Don't be afraid to stop an activity that is getting out of hand and get the text books out – some nice, dry reading to calm everyone down. Students will probably complain, but the point is, they need to *earn* their right to do more exciting activities, through demonstrating that they can do them responsibly.

Identifying the ringleaders

Often, the root cause of problematic group behaviour can be down to one or two individuals, those who have an uncanny way of getting many others involved in their misdemeanours. In short: the ringleaders. Get these students on your side and you may find you have fewer difficulties with the class in general.

The first challenge is to work out who they are. It may be obvious: the ones who have the 'top-dog' reputation around the school or year group, who other students look up to and/or are intimidated by. They'll probably be confident, cocky and unafraid of answering back to anyone who questions their authority (including teachers). Rest assured, as has been previously discussed, this is bravado – underneath it all they'll be highly insecure.

They'll also be intelligent – ringleaders generally are. In this respect, they may not be the loud, clunky, vociferous ones who always seem to be at the centre of trouble, but the quieter ones, who sit on the periphery. Look out for the sly characters who know how to rally everyone up with a few subtle prevarications and then sit back to enjoy the chaos.

Once you have identified your ringleaders, it's a matter of 'taming' them. Don't think of them as your number one rivals. Remember the cliché: keep your friends close and your enemies closer. Tried and tested, one of the most effective ways to tackle the nerve centre of difficult group behaviour is to build a relationship with the chiefs. Take time to talk to them before/after or even outside of lessons. Develop a rapport that sits outside of discipline and work. Give them the sense that you care and recognize their potential. Give them responsibility – feed their egos and channel their 'leadership' skills into more productive pursuits. Ask them to do jobs for you, or to help other students. It may feel like a risk, but the results will be worth it. And for once, you'll be able to be the smug teacher who says, 'Oh, he's never a problem for *me*!'

9 | Getting to grips with general disruption

In this section, I will explore ways of tackling the type of challenging behaviour that can cause significant disruption to a lesson. Such behaviour can be regarded as an extension of the low-level examples discussed, often following similar patterns of attention-seeking, attitude, and restlessness. Low-level problems are generally quite isolated. They are inappropriate, but their main intention is to bother you, or students sitting nearby. Medium-level disruptions, however, have a wider field of influence: remind yourself of the kind of student who goes to any length to court the attention of the entire class. In happy times, he is the loveable class clown; but more frequently, he is the whirlwind of utter destruction.

Work avoidance, attention-seeking, inability to cope with boundaries, lack of self-control. boredom, attention deficit disorders/hyperactivity, low self-esteem, peer pressure: all of these issues can contribute to behaviour that stretches limits and threatens to override your control. However, dealing with this level of behaviour need not be any more daunting than dealing with the low-level issues – it is simply a matter of being prepared and practised, following routines of intervention with calm assertiveness.

Some proactive ideas are outlined below.

Awareness

Discuss the student with other teachers: What types of behaviour do they see? How do they deal with it? What has been effective? Is the student known to have behavioural difficulties, and have they/are they being investigated? What information do you have access to: files, reports, statements, assessments, comments from previous schools? If the student has an Individual Education Plan (IEP), have you seen a copy? To what extent are you involved in setting, monitoring and assessing the IEP targets? Lots of questions, but my point is this: if you are expected to manage students classified with emotional, social and behavioural difficulties, you should be encouraged and supported to become as informed as possible about the specific needs of these individuals. Having this insight will enhance your ability to understand and manage challenge within your classroom (even if it is just for one period a week).

Sometimes this sort of information will not always be automatically passed on to you. You may need to seek it for yourself. I once taught an ESBD student whose exemplary good behaviour outlasted the usual 'honeymoon' period and continued for several months. I had just reached the point of questioning his placement in an ESBD Unit, when his behaviour took a sudden and dramatic nose-dive. His mornings would be stable and jolly, and then, in a Jekyll and Hyde manner, he would mutate after midday. Perplexed by this turn around, I contacted his guardian to see if she had noticed any changes. Two weeks later she got back to me, and said she was worried that she had made a mistake in deciding to lower his Ritalin dose. This was news to me: I had not been informed that the student was taking Ritalin in the first place!

Monitor and identify triggers

If very disruptive behaviour is frequently an issue in your classroom, look at it from a pragmatic point of view. Often the 'whys' and 'hows' of behaviour can be explained (whether or not they can be excused). Focusing your attention on looking for explanations may be the key to overcoming the difficulties. Spend some time (a few weeks/half a term) carefully monitoring the events unfolding in your classroom – do things as you would usually do them, but be reflective. If everything goes wrong, so be it – your aim is to work out why it went wrong. Look for patterns of behaviour:

1   When do problems occur (after break; at the start of a lesson/end of lesson; transitional periods/unstructured times; during quiet, individual work; carpet time)?
2   What are the triggers (interaction with certain students; comments from other students; particular tasks; group activities; boredom)?
3   If you confront the student, how do they react?
4   In what way does your response to the student affect the outcome?
5   What seems to have a positive affect (your approach; humour; peer pressure; change of task)?

Once you have gathered information, analyse it. Some surprisingly obvious signs may emerge. For example, behavioural difficulties may frequently occur at the start of individual work, resulting in the student avoiding the entire task. Perhaps the student has strong insecurities about their writing skills and uses disruptive behaviour as a way to deflect attention from this. While trying to monitor and gather information of this kind, it is useful to have another set of eyes – for they will be able to see things objectively. They may also be able to keep notes (always helpful to refer back to), and will allow you to concentrate on the rest of your classroom commitments. You may have a support assistant who can do this, or have temporary access to one. There is nothing to stop you requesting some extra support for this purpose. You may wish to set up a collective with other trusted staff members, whereby you take turns to sit in on each other's lessons and support each other in observing and exploring certain aspects of classroom behaviour. If the thought of doing this makes your spine shiver, ask yourself: What have you got to hide?

Tackle causes

If you are able to identify possible triggers for disruptive behaviour you can address the cause of the problem, which will have more long-term benefits than simply dealing with the symptoms. If, for example, difficulties are related to work avoidance or learning needs, you will need to think about differentiating work – making it more accessible, more attractive to the student. You may also need to adjust your expectations of that student's capabilities. If the issue is attention-seeking, then whose attention is being sought? Yours? Other students? How do other class members react to this behaviour – do they laugh and encourage it, or are they fed up of the disruption? It may be worth rearranging the seating plan, or specifying seats for each student. Separate students that aggravate or delight in distracting one another, and, if possible, try to keep them out of each other's sight-line as well (cheeky looks and handsignals can lead to trouble).

If challenging behaviour occurs at certain times of the day, could dietary issues play a part? Too many sugary cans of pop at breaktime, or lack of breakfast causing a mid-morning slump? The excitement of breaktimes can bring students into the classroom with a certain 'high' – allow five minutes' settling time for energy levels to drop before even thinking about starting work.

Sometimes, however, the origins of behaviour will be elusive –

problems may stem from home-life, personal issues or learned behaviour, or the behaviour may be so arbitrary it just seems impossible to determine a trigger. But by eliminating other more measurable possibilities, you can move a few steps towards establishing some clarity about the nature of your problematic students.

Differentiate

A key factor in overcoming disruptive behaviour is the provision of lessons that are suitably absorbing. If students are interested in an idea, or absorbed by an activity, they will be distracted from 'alternative' ways of making life exciting! Work needs to be stimulating and accessible to the whole class, but it also needs to reach the students that fall below common standards.

Differentiation has obvious implications where learning needs are an issue, but can also play a role in motivating reluctant workers. Adjusting the expected level of output, breaking tasks down into smaller chunks, providing structured guideline sheets and vocabulary lists (particularly when large amounts of writing are involved), setting specific and individualized targets can all contribute to making work seem more manageable, and thus more appealing.

I frequently hear teachers saying words to the effect of: 'But he's perfectly capable . . . why doesn't he get on with it like everyone else?' Even when a student is, indeed, capable of completing a task, emotional issues may get in the way. It is easy to assume that a student is simply lazy: but laziness is often a disguise for low self-esteem. The student may fear failing the task, and so avoid attempting it. They may not relate to the purpose of doing it: lack of aspiration. They may not expect to achieve: so why bother at all?

Some students may use work avoidance as a way of 'acting-out' defiance and control, using it to gain attention. Others may have become over-reliant on being nurtured through their learning: if they have received/are receiving small group or one-to-one support, being expected to work independently may take them right out of their comfort zone. These things should be taken into account as you plan your lessons and consider what you want the student to achieve: should they complete a much-resented three-sided essay on Chaucer that makes little sense to them – or to you – and is rich with basic grammatical error? Or should they complete a one-page informative, structured task that maximizes the possibilities of them developing independence and retaining knowledge?

Be prepared

Once again, I wish to emphasize the strength and confidence that can be gained from anticipating difficulties and, more importantly, how they will be handled. As challenging behaviour becomes more serious in its nature, it becomes increasingly important to have a sense of how you will react: thus you will not be leaping frantically from one crisis to another, but will be addressing difficulties in a calm, measured and productive way. Familiarize yourself with early warning signs and patterns: develop a sixth sense for sniffing out trouble. Young people will often give away clues about their state of mind. If a student seems agitated or particularly restless, or there is an unusual amount of chatter coming from one table, investigate. Acting on these signs and intervening early may help prevent a situation from escalating. For example:

'Sally, Janine . . . there seems to be a lot of giggling and whispering coming from your table. If there is a problem, you need to tell me about it – otherwise, I expect you to carry on quietly. I'll be over to see how much work you've done in two minutes . . .'

'Miss, it's not us. Ricky keeps taking our things and getting on our nerves. Tell him, Miss.'

'Thank you for that. Now that you've brought it to my attention, I'm sure Ricky will leave you alone, as he won't want to be speaking with me after the lesson – will you Ricky – which means you girls can work quietly from now on.'

Some reactive ideas are outlined below.

Encourage the rest of the class

A serial troublemaker can invoke varying reactions from the rest of the class: they may be whipped into a frenzy of excitement, they may be passively disinterested, or they may express resentment and frustration – the 'class clown' is not always the most popular student. Unfortunately, when one individual is making a large bid for attention, the rest of the students inevitably miss out. Consider the likelihood that there will be more than one demanding student in a class, and the pressure increases . . . the rigours of inclusion. Ensure that you do what you can to counter this effect by reassuring and encouraging other students in the class. If they are left to their own devices while you deal with a challenging individual, imply that you will be pleased with them if they continue to work quietly (reward them if possible: merits, points?). Acknowledge and praise mature, sensible behaviour. Highlight the fact that you are aware of how difficult it is to concentrate and ignore such disturbances. Not only does this reassure your students that their presence is not being overlooked, but it also reinforces the message that positive attention is awarded to positive behaviour; not so, negative behaviour.

Remain calm and neutral

The tone of your voice can have a significant effect on the outcome of your interventions. If a student is in an excitable mood, an excitable response (one that is emotionally charged, aggressive or unpredictable) will fuel the fire. If you remain calm, and keep hold of your frustrations for a later time, you are more likely to contain or diffuse the situation. Students with ESBD can have abnormal, excessive reactions to the experiences that you or I may shrug our shoulders at. I shall always remember an incident with a lovely but emotionally damaged young boy who had begun attending a very tightly run mainstream secondary school. Things were going well, until the head of year – a notoriously strict and fearsome person, a man you wouldn't want to undermine – caught this student jokingly jostling his mates in the corridor. The head of year unleashed the sort of telling off that he was infamous for, but I'm sure he never once anticipated the mouthful of abuse he got in return! Consequently, and rather sadly, the boy was excluded.

Raising your voice suddenly can, of course, be a powerful way of gaining attention and expressing the severity of your concern, especially if it is an infrequent occurrence. But it is important to do this without labouring your outpourings with ambiguous or threatening emotional charges: be firm and direct, but neutral. Your aim is to get the best result for everyone involved – the student getting control of their behaviour and complying with your requests; the situation being contained calmly (thus minimizing the impact on you and the rest of the class); the lesson continuing, with respect and dignity still intact. A volatile individual needs calm, controlled intervention as the antidote to their inflamed emotional state. Approach issues in this way and your students will know what you want, but they will also know that you are 'safe'.

Be person-specific

When dealing directly with challenging behaviour, try to be as specific as possible about what you are confronting. If possible, move towards the problem, get down to the student's level and speak directly to them. Refer to the student by name (if necessary, repeat it until you get their attention) and then define the behaviour:

'Asif. Asif. ASIF. You need to stop shouting across the room. It is not fair on the rest of the class, who are trying to concentrate. This is your first warning – I hope it will be your only warning . . . now carry on working quietly please.'

If you have to break your teaching flow to deal with behaviour, pause for a moment before launching your campaign. This gives you a chance to clarify what is going on, and besides, a sudden silence can be a powerful way of getting student attention.

Assert the boundaries

If you use rules or rights in your classroom, they can be useful when tackling difficulties, especially in the primary setting where the teacher has some autonomy over the student's classroom experience. Refer to them when discussing behaviour:

'Sheena. Remember our rule about respect please. We speak politely to each other in this classroom. Thank you.'

If boundaries are frequently reinforced, they will become clearer fixtures in an individual's mind. Repetition increases the likelihood of information being retained – which has added importance when dealing with students who may have conceptual difficulties with interpreting abstract ideas such as the invisible perimeter of expectation, or the link between cause and effect.

Reminding students about the rules/boundaries places emphasis on whole-class expectation. The truth is, not all students will care if *you* are annoyed with them – but they may care about their peers. Therefore, anything that links them to a group mentality can be quite powerful.

Use the language of choice

Using the language of choice will become second nature to your behaviour management skills if practised consistently. Incorporate it into your warnings.

Andrew has been leaning over his desk and flicking another student on the shoulder, distracting him from his work.

'Andrew, this is your first warning – you need to stop winding up Hassan. Face the front of the classroom and get on with your work please.'

A little while later, you spot him at it again.

'Andrew, *you are choosing* to disturb Hassan again – second warning. If you leave him alone and carry on quietly, there will be no more problems. *If you choose* to wind him up further, *you will have* to move to the front of the class – it is up to you. Do you understand?'

Unfortunately, he continues to try to distract Hassan when he thinks you are no longer watching him. Be firm: it is now too late for negotiations, though it is important to emphasize to Andrew that he initially had a chance to turn the situation around. Even if he makes a fuss about moving, you need to dig in your heels. If you back down at this stage, you risk undermining all of your efforts.

'Okay Andrew. You've had two warnings, and you've chosen to continue to bother Hassan. You now need to move to this desk here . . . (he protests) . . . arguing with me won't help – it's your behaviour – you made the choice.'

Or, if Andrew does indeed make the 'right' choice, ensure that you reinforce this with praise.

'Thank you Andrew. It's been 20 minutes since I last had to speak to you, and in that time you've chosen to get on quietly with your work. Well done – you've made a mature decision about your behaviour.'

Be repetitive

Knowing what to say, and how to say it, can feel quite unnatural when you first start teaching or developing your skills, but it does come together with practice. I tend to be quite animated when I am teaching, but if I have to deal with a problem, I automatically switch into behaviour management 'mode'. My voice becomes low and stable. I move towards the problem. I talk through a well-practised series of statements that are designed to give the student choices over their behaviour and its outcomes (see above). It is quite banal – but it works. Using routine and repetition maximizes the potential for students to recognize cause and effect – if they behave inappropriately, then they will receive a certain response, and perhaps a consequence. If, however, they respond to my intervention and improve their behaviour, they will avoid the consequence, and will receive praise for sorting themselves out. Every time an incident occurs this message will be reinforced. Consistency strengthens your wall of behaviour management – if every 'brick' is the same size, and is laid in a similar way, it is harder to break through.

Get attention first

In order to enter a dialogue with an individual about their behaviour, you need to ensure that you have their attention. There is little point in telling a student what they should/should not be doing, if they are simply not listening to you. Think of the times when two or more students are engaged in verbal banter. They are so locked into the frenzy of their 'conversation' that they are oblivious to your presence and your wish to get the lesson started. Before you start to deal with this behaviour, you need to get them to focus on you rather than each other. Your objective is to distract them. Move towards them, stand between them if possible, and repeat the word 'Stop'. Keep repeating it (even if it takes some time) in an assertive, but even tone, until it has the desired effect – from here you can get down to the nitty-gritty. Getting the attention of worked-up students is often infuriating, but if you are persistent and use simple, direct language (the student's name/the word 'stop') it can be overcome.

Remove the problem

If a student starts arguing with another classmate, recognize that this has been triggered by something. Simply telling them to stop arguing will not address the reason for the behaviour. Find out what is at the heart of the problem. If there is significant tension, you may need to discuss this with the students (either together or alone) and negotiate a resolution. If they are not ready to resolve their differences, you may suggest that they revisit the problem after the lesson, and in the meantime remain separated to avoid further disruptions. By being thorough, and identifying/dealing with the trigger of the problem, you reduce the risk of it recurring or escalating.

Remove the student

A single challenging student is one thing, a group of them is another matter. There is always a risk that an excitable individual will take others down with them. Some will be dragged; others will go willingly. If other class members are finding it difficult to control their reactions to a challenging individual, or are at risk of getting sucked into disruptive behaviour, your priority should be to remove the nucleus/nuclei.

1   Tackle the student who is at the source of the disturbance and get them away from the rest of the students. Send them outside, or to a lonely corner of the classroom – a space where they can calm down, without an audience to entertain.
2   Inform the student that you will speak to them when they are calmer. But be prepared: once removed, they may continue trying to court attention – faces at the window, ridiculous noises – further intervention may be necessary.
3   Now is your time to focus on the rest of the class: advise them to make a responsible choice about their own behaviour and discourage them from looking at/responding to/encouraging the offending student. Like a shepherd herding his flock, you will need to draw your students back into your fold. Prioritize getting them back on task. Praise those who have ignored the difficulties, and speak to any students who have become carried away themselves. Praise them if they have managed to pull themselves back.
4   Once the class is settled again, you can turn your attention to the student at the source of the problem. Hopefully, they will have

calmed down, and from there it is a matter of establishing whether they acknowledge the unacceptable nature of their behaviour, whether they are prepared to put things right and whether they are ready/committed to re-entering the classroom and working sensibly.

5 Depending on the seriousness of the incident and their subsequent manner, you may decide that it is more appropriate for them to take their work to another class or to the deputy head's office, thus giving you and your class the chance to move on.

Some follow-up ideas are outlined below.

Seek the positive

For your own peace of mind, if no one else's, off-load your frustrations about the challenging individuals in your classes. If you are putting up an unaffected, unshaken front throughout the day, you need to have somewhere to vent your true feelings. Sharing anecdotes with colleagues (things often seem humorous with hindsight), and ranting to your friends and family about the *unbelievable* things you put up with, is all good for your soul. But try not to dwell on negative interpretations of events, for the sake of your morale. Tell yourself that it is not your fault if students bring problematic behaviour to your classroom. Praise yourself for the fact that you are one of the extraordinary people in the world who is prepared to face up to this challenge. Remind yourself that an individual is so much more than a catalogue of behavioural difficulties: think around the problems.

Focus on the good qualities that your challenging students may possess. Perhaps they are caring, or enthusiastic. Maybe they like responsibility, or have particular talents. If good qualities are well hidden, try looking for possibilities within the negative characteristics: in other circumstances these behaviours may be very useful – an argumentative student has determination and opinions. A student that frequently shows off may make a confident performer. A devious student will make a good politician.

The conversation

If you have chosen to send a student for some time-out (either in or out of the classroom), you will, at some point, have to re-engage with them in order to address the problem and determine how and when they are to return to the lesson. You need to have a conversation about the situation: how you do this can have a significant effect on the outcome. First, you need to establish two things: that the student is calm enough to talk appropriately, and that you are calm enough to talk appropriately. If you screech with fury, the student is unlikely to give the response you want. If they, on the other hand, have failed to regain some self-control, they will not be ready to see reason. Before you start to make negotiations, you need to see evidence of calmer behaviour. If necessary, give the student more time, or assist them (some students need personal space to sort themselves out, others may benefit from adult intervention). Whether they are in a silly mood or an angry mood, inform them that they need to show more responsible behaviour before they are able to return to class.

When having 'the conversation' your aims are to:

1 Clarify the facts.
2 Encourage the student to take ownership.
3 Establish a resolution.
4 Consider what could be done next time.

Ask the student to look at you as you speak to them – if they struggle to do this with sincerity, then they are perhaps not ready to return to class (some students may have genuine difficulty maintaining eye contact so request it with sensitivity). State the reason why they have been sent outside and check they understand that the particular behaviour was inappropriate, and why it was inappropriate. Whenever possible, ask the student for the answers rather than giving them away – encourage reflection. Give the student an opportunity to explain why they did it. Ask them what they could do to put the situation right (make any necessary apologies, make up for missed work, make more effort?). Ask them what they might do if they have a similar problem in the future (talk to an adult, move away from the problem, ask for help?). If you are satisfied with the responses, thank them for having a mature discussion with you, and remind them that you expect to see that same level of maturity throughout the rest of the lesson.

Dig for guilt

Although I discourage emotionally charged responses when dealing with challenging students (e.g. anger, impatience, personal dislike, power-seeking), there are times when it is fruitful to display a human side. Letting a student know that you have been affected negatively by their behaviour can give them a good dose of guilt. Feeling guilty, feeling bad, is a way of knowing our actions are unhelpful and unacceptable. Sometimes it can be exceedingly difficult to get students with emotional difficulties to reconcile with this response – the child that never seems to show genuine remorse, or cannot empathize. However, if you have developed an otherwise positive relationship with a difficult student, expressing personal disappointment regarding their negative behaviour (reminding them that you believe that they are capable of better things) can be very effective. I recall keeping half of my class back at breaktime to deal with a minor bullying incident. I laid it on thick:

> 'I am *so* upset that boys in this class have chosen to behave in this way. Throughout the year you have shown me what a considerate, thoughtful group of people you can be – so I am very surprised, and disappointed, to learn that this has been going on. It makes me feel very sad.'

After ten minutes, there were tears (not mine) . . . and no more bullying – for a few weeks, at least!

Expect sincerity

In retribution for an incident of challenging behaviour you may wish to be given an apology from a student as an acknowledgement of the inappropriateness of their actions. Incorporate the expectation of this apology into the routine of your incident follow-up (see 'The conversation' above). If practised consistently, it can provide an anchoring starting point for establishing the consequences of a student's behaviour. It also teaches students to face up to their own actions, to admit mistakes and to communicate more effectively. When asking for an apology, encourage the student to address you personally, and to explain exactly what they are sorry for: make them think through their actions, and actually relate these to the apology they are giving. (This is equally important when they are giving apologies to other people they may have bothered.)

Though simple by design, an adequate apology can be a very hard thing to give – thus it is often a very powerful consequence in itself. For it to be effective, however, it has to be sincere. Obtaining 'sorry' words from a student is one thing. Obtaining true, heart-felt words is another. If you sense that an individual is making a joke of the request, or simply going through the motions just to get back into class and cause more mayhem – explain that they have not got it right yet:

> 'I'm afraid, Wendy, I just don't feel you really mean these words. You're not looking at me, you're smirking to yourself, you're slouching against the wall and messing about with the radiator . . . but you need to be showing me that you are ready to come back to class. I will give you an opportunity to try the apology again, and this time I want you to stand up straight, look at me, and really think about what you are saying . . .'

Of course, giving an apology in the right way is not always a guarantee that it *is* truly meant; but it does mean that the individual is prepared to toe your line of expectation.

There is a certain kind of student who never seems to learn from their mistakes. They may be adept at apologizing for misbehaviour, but will quickly repeat the cycle. In this instance, I have a favourite phrase: 'you use the word "sorry", but how can you *show me* that you are sorry?'. In context:

> 'Paul, saying sorry is not very effective anymore, is it? You've said it many times, and then disturbed the class again. I'm not prepared to accept your apologies anymore until you start showing me that you really mean it. How do you think you can show me this? . . . Yes. By *changing* your behaviour, by trying not to do those things anymore. You need to make a much bigger effort . . . I shall be looking out for the effort you are making, and if I see it, I shall be pleased. But if I don't see improvements then I will have to speak to your head of year . . .'

Accept sincerity

If a student makes an earnest apology, accept it with good grace, thank them and explain that you appreciate their maturity. Given that owning behaviour is an important aspect of becoming a more responsible individual, it is important that you support any effort to do this. I feel I have to make this point, because I have often observed situations that undermine this. As an example: an ESBD student had become agitated and disruptive during a lesson and had to be removed by senior staff. It was a fairly serious matter, but it was dealt with, and the student spent most of the rest of the day outside the head of year's office, in tearful, humble regret. Deciding the boy had served his time the head of year led him to the staffroom to make an apology to the teacher whose lesson had been disturbed. The boy gave a very genuine apology, but in return was yelled at. The phrase 'I don't ever want him back in my class' was actually used! While I understand the stress that challenging students can impose on staff, reacting in this way can only make the situation harder, and do further damage to fragile relationships.

(A thought: if a student is being brought to you to give an apology, it is perhaps fair that you are given some prior warning, allowing you to compose yourself and prepare your response.)

10 | Dealing with students who refuse to cooperate

One of the key obstacles to success with challenging behaviour is the will of the individual. You give a perfectly reasonable request to a student, and they go out of their way not to do it. To me, this has always defied logic: why make life difficult for yourself? But then I have to remember that I don't have the mindset of a troubled young person. I do not fear having control taken from me. I do not get confused by conflicting boundaries. And I do not have deep anxieties about what my friends think of me. I do what I'm told . . . but only if I'm asked nicely.

Refusal (deliberately not following instructions), defiance ('no one tells me what to do'), avoidance (running away, pretending not to listen) and being obtuse (sulking, arguing back) are the uncooperative symptoms of the student who hates to have power taken from them. If they feel their sense of self/power is threatened, they will employ their well-tuned defence mechanism: lack of cooperation. If they are telling you that you cannot tell them what to do, they are right.

You will not win the battle of wills if trying to overcome power with power. An emotionally disturbed, wound-up, tense and angry young person is probably more desperate to keep the upper hand than you are. Approaching the situation in an overbearing way is likely to lead to further confrontation. Instead, you should aim to diffuse the pressure on yourself and the student by stepping back from behaviour, allowing time and space for the student to reflect, and then revisiting the problem when the atmosphere has settled. I am not suggesting that refusal to follow instructions should be tolerated, but that it will benefit from sensitive handling.

Some proactive ideas are outlined below.

Be a fair player

If you have established a reputation among your classes as a teacher who is reasonable and respectful towards your students, your expectations are less likely to be challenged. There are teachers who have strong discipline, but are generally disliked. There are teachers who are well liked, but have weak discipline. Alas, there are some that fail on both counts; but there are also those who are well-liked by their students and can still maintain good order. The two factors go hand in hand: if you develop *positive* discipline, you will be liked. If you are liked, your students will want to cooperate with you. Of course, this is a simplistic vision, but it represents the root of effective and meaningful behaviour management – your starting point should always be the establishment of a positive, trusting relationship. Being blessed with a dynamic personality may help in the popularity stakes, but true respect is derived from being consistently fair and firm.

Use techniques that offer a way out

If you consistently offer your students options when dealing with behaviour (see 'Use the language of choice' on p. 66), they will know that your intentions are not to back them into a corner and overpower them. Likewise, allowing students personal space in which to calm down (a designated area of the classroom, or outside) can ease the tension that is derived from feeling crowded in. If your behaviour management style provides students with alternatives to rising conflict, and offers them the opportunity to get themselves out of a difficult situation, it will impact on those individuals who deeply resent following orders.

One of my students would routinely refuse to start a task – any attempt to encourage or get him started would result in a protracted argument and sulking. He was a capable student, but had a very negative view of his abilities and would try to control and manipulate his situation in order to waste time and avoid facing this insecurity. If, however, he was given a simple, quick briefing: 'this is what I expect you to do . . . Do the work in the lesson, or you will have to do it in your own time. You make the choice', and then left to his own devices, he would spend the first ten minutes with his head on his desk, quietly aware of the praise and attention that other students were receiving for their efforts. Then, eventually, he would pick up his pen and start working with enthusiasm and care. Ironically, he would then refuse to stop!

Recognize serious situations

Sometimes it is possible, and perhaps more appropriate, to walk away from a student (both literally and metaphorically) who is refusing to follow instructions. If the trigger and circumstances of the incident are low-level (i.e. having limited impact on the rest of the class) then let the individual have their own space. Simply inform them that if they choose not to follow your requests, then they will need to speak with you at the end of class. However, you may be working with students that have very short fuses when under pressure (remember, it is important to know the background of your students and their behavioural difficulties), or the situation may be disrupting the entire class. In these circumstances, it is necessary to deal with the matter as quickly as possible, even if it means temporarily stopping the session. You do not want your entire lesson consumed by one individual; and you do not want to expose yourself or other students to the risk of aggressive outbursts. Also, it is vital that serious disruption is seen by other students to be taken seriously. Use your better judgement and act accordingly.

Know your school's policy on runners

Flight or fight: some students will respond to pressure by confronting it with aggression, others will run away. You may work with students who have a tendency to storm out of class, or leave a designated area, if they perceive themselves as being victimized. If the student has left the classroom, can you be accountable for their behaviour? What if they then go and disturb other classes? Are they safe? Are they still within the school walls? If they leave the building, should parents be contacted? The police? The same applies to the type of student that *relishes* escaping from your clutches: the type who cannot cope with a structured, boundary-defined environment, and resorts to immature silliness that invariably results in running from responsibility.

Runners place you in a compromizing position: you will not want to leave the rest of the class unattended, but at the same time you may feel unpleasantly responsible for the individual who has absconded. It is important for schools to have a united policy on dealing with students who leave designated areas without permission, thus teachers in this position need not feel stranded or neglectful. Procedures will vary, so ensure that you are familiar with the way your school does things. In general, I would suggest that if a student runs away, you should alert the office/senior staff, either by phone or by sending a student messenger, and the matter can be organized from there. If you work in a smaller school, or in a primary school, you may have more direct responsibility. You may need to enlist the aid of a support worker/nearby teacher to mind your class, while you track down the student yourself.

Some reactive ideas are outlined below.

Remain calm

When a student is going out of their way to defy you, it can feel very frustrating. Moreover, it can feel like a threat to your ability to control the class. You don't want the conflict to escalate, yet you don't want to give in. Above all, you don't want the rest of the class thinking you're a soft touch. These issues will contribute to the stress of the situation. If you are stressed, you are more likely to resort to erratic, confrontational methods of management, which will lead to further problems. Take a deep breath. Keep calm. Remind yourself that the student is making the moment difficult, not because they want to get at you, but because they have deep-rooted insecurities about themselves. Even when a student is being cocky and arrogant, let it wash over you, you can pick up on rudeness later. Right now, your priority is to not rise to their bait.

Emphasize choice

Choice encourages responsible decision-making. Choice also allows you to step out of the conflict equation: the source of the problem is from within the student. It is not a result of your unreasonable demands:

> 'Okay, Steven. You're choosing not to take a time-out. In other words, you're choosing not to follow my instructions. I will give you a minute to think about this, and hopefully in that time you will decide to make the right choice . . . If you do the time-out, then that will be the end of the issue. If you choose not to, then I'm afraid there will have to be a further consequence: you may have to lose your breaktime.'

Make sure that the choices you provide are clear and unambiguous – keep it simple. Too many options or comments that are vague in intention will confuse rather than help the individual. Also, ensure that the student is fully aware that they *do* have choice – an agitated individual may not be listening or thinking very clearly, and could easily misinterpret vital information. I can recall countless times where students have started needlessly huffing and puffing, assuming that they have received a consequence, when in fact it has merely been suggested.

Give the student space

A common complication in the classroom environment is patience, or rather impatience. Due to the considerable pressures that have to be addressed, there is an urge to want everything done there and then: come in, sit down, be quiet, DO IT NOW. The reality is that some students will take time to follow instructions, especially if they are not keen to follow them. Students who have issues with cooperation may create additional problems. It is tempting to lose patience in these circumstances, and try to menace the student(s) into coercion – however this approach is very likely to lead to further conflict, and thus waste even more time.

If a student is behaving in a defiant manner, resist the temptation to shout them down. Give a clear, direct statement about what you would like them to do/what choices they have, and then give them some time to think it through. It is helpful if you can be specific about the amount of time (one minute, three minutes), and, if appropriate, provide visual prompts – a stopwatch or an egg timer. Leave the individual to mull things over in their own space and focus on the rest of the class.

You may find that, with pressure and expectation removed, students takes it upon themselves to 'make the right choice' within the set time limit. Avoid drawing attention to this immediately (they will probably be feeling a little raw with shame), but be sure to acknowledge that you are pleased that they made a good, mature decision before the lesson is through. If you get to the end of the specified time, and the student is still sour-faced, then inform them that you are sorry they made an unhelpful choice and that they will have to face the consequence of that.

You may be presented with a situation in which a student refuses to do what you have asked them to do, yet remains smugly quiet and continues working ('Leave me alone . . . I'm getting on with my work.'); this is power-seeking behaviour in another disguise. It is not worth battling over. Simply inform them that you are happy to see that they are getting on with things. but that they will, however, need to speak with you at the end of the lesson about refusing to follow instructions.

If it gets serious

Christopher repeatedly makes silly noises while you are trying to talk to the class. He ignores three warnings and then refuses to accept a sobering time-out. It is as though he is actively pushing to be in as much trouble as possible, and the chances are, he is. If a young person has grown up within a cycle of misbehaviour and punishment, they may find comfort there: familiar territory. They may not be used to behaviour management methods that require them to take responsibility for their actions, or give them the chance to put things right. Why? Impatient adults that resort to yelling, threatening, cursing, aggressive responses in order to get some 'peace and quiet'. Christopher is loudly refusing to leave the class-room, making cocky remarks and relishing the moment. You are concerned that his behaviour is distracting the rest of the class and threatening to undermine your position. Steer the rest of your students away from the situation:

'Class. Unfortunately, one of our group is having difficulties following instructions – no one else needs to get involved, thank you Gary. I don't wish to see your hard work interrupted, so I would like you to carry on quietly by yourselves for a moment – read through the rest of the worksheet and answer questions one to five . . . that will be really helpful. Merits for those of you that get through it all.'

Reduce the audience as much as possible (showing off is pretty pointless when no one is looking) and then have a firm, quiet word with the difficult student:

'Christopher, I've asked you several times to take a time-out and you know why this is, you made that choice for yourself. The rest of the class are wanting to get on with the lesson, and so do I. You need to take some time-out now, then I will come and speak to you again . . .'

Hopefully, with the pressure of class interest reduced, Christopher will be able to accept the consequence. If not, the matter goes to the next level . . .

Call for back-up

'Christopher, you need to take the time-out or I will have to get the deputy head involved – unfortunately I can't spend any more class time with you right now if you are refusing to co-operate. I'll give you one more chance to think about this: would you rather you and I deal with the problem together, or do you want senior staff on your back? Take a time-out or get into trouble with the deputy?'

All schools should have senior/experienced members of staff available to deal with major behaviour problems or student extraction. Make sure you know the system for getting in contact with them (either by phone, or by trusted student messenger). It is, of course, important that you deal with as much behaviour as you can by yourself. Not only is this good for your own confidence, but it is essential to your reputation among the students that they see you as someone who is not afraid of confronting problematic behaviour. However, there are times when it is absolutely necessary to engage the assistance of others: if a student has refused to cooperate with you at every level of intervention; if a student is being extremely and continuously disruptive and ignoring instructions to do otherwise; and if a student seems particularly agitated or aggressive and you have concerns about violent/abusive behaviour. Call for support before a situation gets out of hand, bearing in mind it may take a while to arrive. If it never arrives (I only say this because it once happened to me), there will hopefully be colleagues working in nearby rooms who can help.

While you are waiting, and if it is safe to do so, step back from the situation and attend to the rest of the class – do not push the problem further. When help arrives, explain the problem using the same language, tone and expressions that you would use when talking directly to the student ('Hello, sir. Nice to see you. Unfortunately you're here because Christopher has made some really unhelpful choices about his behaviour today, and is refusing to cooperate . . .'). Be transparent. I have watched students get extremely riled when they see adults talking about them in ways that they perceive to be secretive or conspiratorial.

Remove the class

There may be times when even the intervention of senior staff will not budge an obstinate student. Your options are to forcibly remove the student, or remove the class. Removing the student will be less upheaval for the class, but could be difficult to execute. There may be a backlash to such personal handling: tables being kicked over, physical altercations. More than one adult may be required to assist in the removal, and they will certainly need to be trained for this kind of intervention. Removing the class, on the other hand, may be logistically tricky, but safer and less intrusive overall. Not only this, but it can have a powerful effect on the problematic student. Being taken away is tough, but also quite exciting and sensational. There is nothing like being left behind – all alone with a couple of stern teachers – to give you a grim, cold reality-check.

Some follow-up ideas are outlined below.

Talk through the issue

Imagine that you have tackled refusing behaviour and are carrying on with your lesson – at some point you will need to discuss the behaviour with the student. Perhaps you have requested to speak to them after class, or are following up a time-out. Explain to the student that instructions are there to help them and if they follow them they could avoid getting into further trouble:

> 'You don't like being told what to do, do you Liam?'
> 'Nah miss.'
> 'No. Not many people do. But in some situations we all have to learn to follow instructions in order to get anywhere. If I give you an instruction, Liam, it is because I know it will be helpful to you. If I ask you to take a time-out, it's not a punishment – it's so that you can have some time to yourself, to calm down and think about what you're doing. But if you refuse to take that help, then you're not cooperating with me, and that becomes a serious matter, because lack of cooperation is going to cause problems for the whole class. Do you understand?'

Emphasize the absolute importance of cooperation.

Put consequences in place

Uncooperative, defiant behaviour can often be secondary to an original problem: a stress response to being disciplined. You now have two issues: the consequence of the original inappropriate behaviour, and the consequence of refusing to follow instructions. In the heat of the moment, deal with the immediate behaviour (refusal). The original problem can be dealt with later.

When talking through the situation with the student (either after class or before you let them back into class), be sure to clarify what the consequences are and what they are for. You may wish to see the student make up the time that was wasted while they were refusing to cooperate: ten-minute detention at breaktime/catch-up work handed to you tomorrow morning (consider whether this consequence is realistic for the student with a poor work record). You may also wish to define a consequence for the problem that led up to the refusing behaviour: for example, a student has thrown screwed-up paper across the room then refused to pick it up – they can spend the ten-minute detention tidying up.

Consequences need to be meaningful, realistic and appropriate. It is not necessarily the scale of the consequence, but the chord that it strikes: ten minutes at lunch (when they could be hanging out with their mates) can be more effective than five sides of lines (which they get their mates to help them with anyway). If keeping a student in, or holding a detention, don't be tempted to have a laugh and a chat with them. It undermines the point of the sanction. Either give them an activity (not a fun one) or have them sit in silence.

Show forgiveness

Explain to your students and, if necessary, remind yourself, that once consequences have been completed and apologies made, the slate is wiped clean. The next lesson will be an opportunity for the student to prove how lovely they really are . . . yeah right. Sometimes it can be difficult to let go of the resentment and frustration created by students who deliberately defy you and make classroom life difficult. And if it happens on a regular basis there may be little space left for the 'everyone deserves a second chance' theory! I'm sure most staff members can identify with that sinking feeling: the anticipation of teaching certain classes containing certain students. Although solace may be found in bitching to colleagues, there will always be someone with a waspish face saying: 'Well he's fine in my lessons.'

The problem is, if a student senses that you are uncomfortable with them, it is likely that they will become even more unco-operative. It is so important to keep emotional responses to your students, and their natures, in check. Individuals with ESBD can be surprisingly perceptive, and will quickly pick up on vibes. They can also be very manipulative (not because they are evil, but because this is how they have learned to cope with life). They will use your reactions and vulnerabilities against you. Your best defence when working with challenging students is emotional indifference. If this feels false, bear in mind that effective behaviour management is no more than a skilful piece of acting.

A step too far: tackling high-level disruption and aggression

In the following chapters I will focus on the management of the kind of problems that pose very serious threats to classroom order: aggressive, abusive and violent behaviour. Although having a solid grasp of general management of challenging students will prevent many situations from escalating, there may still be occasions when difficulties develop too rapidly to contain. Sadly, there will also be students who have confrontational behaviour so deeply ingrained in them that it may be their first response to anything.

First, I will explore the issue of verbal abuse, with regards to insults directed at you (the teacher), and insults hurled between students. Second, I will discuss the issue of physical aggression, focusing initially on the common problem of fighting between students, followed by the less frequent, but extremely serious, issue of physical assault on staff.

Aggressive, abusive behaviour has no simple solutions, partly because its origins are so profoundly complex. The sad reality is that many children exhibiting persistent violent or unpleasant behaviour will have grown up in violent, unpleasant environments. Unless this issue can be addressed, violence will manifest in these young people, and will be brought into schools. Schools may struggle to contain students with extreme emotional, social and behavioural needs. This is not necessarily a sign of weakness: they simply do not have the specific expertise, time, resources and flexibility that such individuals require. They also have a duty to ensure the safety of staff and other students – thus a hard line needs to be drawn against aggression.

Whether you feel that aggressive, abusive behaviour is a risk in your classroom or not, it pays to be prepared. Coping with verbal or physical issues requires the same kind of calm assertiveness that is used to deal with less serious incidents, though naturally it becomes harder to retain a sense of calmness when your nerves are being pushed to their limits.

11 | Dealing with verbal abuse

Verbal abuse to yourself

A student has produced a canned drink, opened it and blatantly started drinking during your lesson. You've been reasonable:

> 'You know that drinking in class is not acceptable, Leon. You need to bring it to me and I will keep it safe. If there are no more problems, you can have it back at the end of the lesson . . . Keeping it on your desk is not an option.'

He responds by putting his feet up and taking a long, leisurely swig from the can. You give him another warning and he gracefully gives you the finger. Some of the class laugh nervously. Some of them make that 'ooooh' sound, watching to see what you will do next.

> 'That kind of rudeness, Leon, is not acceptable in this class-room. You need to take some time-out and I will speak to you again in five minutes.'

He heads for the door with a ridiculously arrogant swagger, making sure that he gets the last word: 'Yeah . . . and I f*cked your mum last night.'

Charming. But however rude, vulgar or spiteful, verbal abuse directed at you need not undermine your position. Pull back from power-seeking, pull back from emotional reactions – just be firm (loud, if necessary), and go through the motions with calm assertiveness.

Step One: Take a deep breath, get in touch with your inner smile, and assess

Encountering verbal abuse or rudeness is utterly infuriating. Especially when it is delivered with calculated poise: the culprit is trying to press your buttons, undermine you and humiliate you. Rudeness does not necessarily have to be a long list of expletives. It can be quietly nasty: 'You can't teach . . . you're useless' is easily more disheartening than a random 'dickhead'. If the rest of the class is watching with bated breath, the situation can feel very pressurized. Your instincts may tell you to keep the upper hand, shout back and demonstrate your power, but this is the least helpful thing you could do. Conflict arising from the need to retain power is the fuel that feeds the fire. Instead of taking the intended offence, quickly assess the situation and put verbal attitude into context. Your aim is to defy confrontation and rise above the insults – shout, scream and kick all you like in the sanctuary of the staff room, but for now, keep your dignity.

Step Two: Intervene at the appropriate level

If the student seems aggressive, there may be a risk of further threatening behaviour, thus your priority will be to have them leave the vicinity of your classroom, either by taking a time-out or joining another class. Firmly request that they take time-out/go next door/wait outside/etc., but keep it simple: 'Vicky, you know that comment is not appropriate in this classroom. You need to take a time-out and calm down.' Repeat the instruction if necessary, but do not let emotions creep in. If she refuses to leave the room, she is moving into the territory of 'uncooperative behaviour' (discussed in the previous chapter). Remain neutral and do not take any effort to defy you, undermine you, or piss you off, personally.

If you determine that the student is being 'cheeky', or provocative without aggression, you may prefer to contain them in the classroom. Let them know that their comments are unacceptable, but remain unbothered (do you really care what rat-boy thinks of your fashion sense?). If appropriate, disarm the culprit with humour, 'I'm honoured that you have such strong opinions about me, Gary!'. If a student seems agitated or upset with you (the one that sulkily mutters 'bitch' under their breath when they've been told off), surprise them with sympathy:

'Paul, if you have a problem, I'll happily discuss it with you after the lesson – but otherwise, let's just concentrate on our work.'

If the insult is particularly offensive, sexist, or racist, it is advisable to treat it seriously. In the first instance send the student for time-out, which will you give you an opportunity to collect your thoughts before tackling the issue directly.

Step Three: Seek an apology

If a verbal insult has gone too far, the problem will need to be addressed. First, an apology would be appropriate. You may choose to elicit this from the student yourself while they are taking time-out away from an audience, and once they have had some time to calm down. Do not try to drag an apology out of a student who is still too angry, hyper or silly to deliver it sincerely. Give them more time (warn them that they will have to make up the time if they cannot compose themselves quickly) or give them some assistance. An angry individual may need some support in calming down: speak in a low, steady voice and express empathy:

'I can see that you are feeling angry – but if you calm down then you can explain why you've become so upset with me – I'd like us to sort this out . . .'

A silly individual, on the other hand, needs the influence of stern reason:

'Sort yourself out! Stand up straight and look at me please – you need to show some maturity and think about your behaviour . . .'

Make sure you get the sincere apology *before* you invite the student back into the classroom, otherwise you may see a repeat performance once they have their audience again.

If a student has verbally insulted you because they have been upset, ensure that you give them an opportunity to explain their version of events. A textbook example:

'Amanda, I don't appreciate the comments you made to me. They broke our rule about respectful behaviour towards one another. Can you explain why you said those things?'
    'Cos you wouldn't let me go on the Internet.'
    'OK. Why did I not want you to go on the Internet?'
    'I dunno . . .'

'Think about it – do I let students use the Internet whenever they please?'

'No? Well – then why do you think I should have let you use it?'

'It's not fair – I NEVER get to go on the Internet!'

'Right. I allow students to use the Internet as a reward for good work and behaviour – if you want a chance to use it, then you need to think about that. I tell you what . . . if you make a special effort to work hard and be polite, I'll make sure that you go on my Internet list. But remember, you need to make a special effort, and you need to start by putting things right with me. How do you think you can do that?'

'By saying sorry . . .'

'Yeah. That will help. So . . .'

'I'm sorry Miss.'

'What are you sorry for?'

'I'm sorry for calling you a bitch . . .'

'Thank you for that. I appreciate your apology. But you now need to show me that you really mean those words. So what are you going to do when you go back into class?'

'Be nice to you . . .'

'Okay. If I notice that you are making a really special effort to avoid saying things that might be disrespectful to others – not just to me, but everyone in the class – then I'll know that you are sorry, and I'll be pleased with you for making a positive effort. Remember – you're trying to get onto my Internet list! Right, let's go back into class now.'

If the incident has been serious (aggressive or highly offensive), you should seek the support of another adult when attempting a conciliatory discussion, or at least be certain that the student will respond appropriately. A third party can often provide a neutral influence which will diffuse the pressure and tension of a one-to-one conversation.

Step Four: Apply further consequences

It may be felt that, in addition to an apology, further consequences will be necessary, but make sure they are issued for their meaningfulness – not revenge. An effective consequence in this respect is a phone-call home:

'Hi . . . Mrs Nesbitt? This is Kieran's class teacher. I felt I ought to let you know that, unfortunately, Kieran has made some very inappropriate comments in class today . . . (cue a lengthy conversation about Kieran's wild ways at home) . . . well, it was good to talk to you Mrs Nesbitt. Hopefully next time we have a conversation, it will be good news about Kieran's progress.'

If comments have been sexist or racist you will need to check your school's policy on dealing with such issues. Seek advice from other staff about who should be informed.

Step Five: Reflect

As with all aspects of behaviour management, it can be helpful to analyse your experiences of verbal abuse and look at how the incidents may have come about. Identify triggers, and be prepared to consider your influence over events. Be honest, be reflective and learn from the experience. Unreasonable expectations, curtness before it's due, snapping at students, seeming like you're fed up of them, a hostile manner – your attitude creates an atmosphere. There is a fine line between firmness and impatience, but it is important to be on the right side of that line. If you are not calm and reasonable, can you honestly expect your students to be calm and reasonable?

Verbal abuse between students

It is important that you take action on unpleasant comments between students, as they undermine one of the key principles of an effective classroom environment: respect. Monitoring the inter-relations of an entire class is not an easy process. Your vigil will be aided if you have additional support staff; otherwise keep alert and prioritize early intervention. Small initial steps may prevent a situation from escalating. Be aware of likely problem areas: a couple of volatile students seated near each other may need a bit more vigilance than the 'good' table. If you take responsibility for the seating arrangements in your classroom, look at ways of separating the potential problems in advance. If you become aware of comments that are beginning to resemble a slanging match between students, act swiftly. This sort of interaction can quickly escalate and has the potential to become physical.

Students with ESBD can be famed for their efforts to deliberately aggravate and wind-up other people. If you are frequently confronted with situations involving such a student being unpleasant towards other class members, you may need to remind yourself: they are not a nasty piece of work, just very unskilled at relating to their fellow humans. Sadly, anti-social behaviour of this kind can often exclude ESBD students from the very kinds of experiences that they would benefit from: group activities, trips, opportunities to build social skills and raise self-esteem. Alienation reinforces a poor self-image. As a teacher you may be able to make a difference if you endeavour to accept the student who goes out of their way to repel people. Deal with the inappropriate or unpleasant behaviour, but also focus on developing a positive relationship with the student. It is more likely that they will heed your instruction if they feel you have a genuine interest in their welfare and are willing to give them a chance.

Step One: Interrupt and separate

Whether the banter is taking place across the classroom, or between students sat next to one another, your aim is to get between them and get their attention. Physical presence is key, especially when verbal requests to calm down might be ignored or ineffective. Move into the middle, or in front of the crossfire, and, if necessary, get down to student eye-level. Command them to 'stop' very firmly, and loudly. Just repeat this until you get a response: your priority at this stage is simply to distract them. As soon as you get their attention, separate them before they have a chance to pipe up again:

> 'Angelo, come and speak to me please. Darren, you need to stay seated and I will speak with you when I have finished with Angelo. The rest of you can carry on working quietly. Please don't get involved with other people's problems.'

If one, or both, students are very agitated, they will need to take some time to calm down before they are able to address the problem. Offer them time-out (in separate locations) and then check up on them. Remember though, some individuals may need the support and reassurance of another adult in order to calm down. Judge whether this is necessary and, if so, who can provide it. Are you in a position to leave your class temporarily, or can a support assistant take responsibility? Do you need to call for further assistance?

Step Two: Gather information

Depending on the level of aggression and agitation, you may choose to take Angelo outside the door. If appropriate, speak to him in the classroom so you will not have to leave other students unattended. Seek privacy: an area of the room where Angelo will not be able to catch the eye of other students vying to wind him up. Your objective is to calm him down and find out what has caused the problem: 'Right. I need you to calmly tell me what has happened . . .'. It is possible that you will get a barrage of information. Ensure that you get clarification of two key points: the student's perception of the ill that has been done to them ('He stole my fags/called my sister a slag/said his mates are gonna get me after school'); and also their perception of the ill that they have dished out in return ('I didn't say nuffink to him/said his mum was a fat bitch/told him to watch out').

Bearing in mind that you may not always be able to solve the root of a problem (particularly if the argument relates to circumstances beyond the classroom), with information about who said what to who, you will at least be able to directly address this evidence. Gather corresponding information from the other student, explaining to both of them that you will listen to each of their stories before making any judgements. Emphasize that both students will be given a fair hearing: there is nothing more likely to thwart progress than the perceived injustice of teachers!

Step Three: Address the problem

Once you have obtained a clear picture of what has happened, you need to determine what action will be taken. The problem may need to be addressed head-on or shelved. If the cause of the argument is straightforward ('He took my pencil') then the solution is geared towards returning the pencil to its rightful owner, or if that cannot be agreed upon, the teacher keeping the pencil until the situation can be conveniently revisited. But arguments are often more complicated than that, especially if they relate to the wider circumstances of a young person's life: 'His sister stole my sister's boyfriend'-type stuff. Lesson time is not suited to unravelling the intricacies of such problems. Invite the students to discuss the issue at the end of class/breaktime, assure them that you will happily help them to deal with the problem, but explain that choosing to argue in lessons will lead to consequences. So for now they need to find a way of getting on in class without creating problems for each other. They may need to be seated separately: emphasize that this is not a punishment, but a way of helping them to avoid further trouble.

If verbal insults have been particularly offensive, racist, or sexist, or if you suspect that bullying may be an underlying factor, you will need to treat the matter seriously. Make it clear to the students that this is the case, and be explicit about how you will be following up the matter: for example, talking to their tutor / head of year, speaking to their parents. In such circumstances, the inappropriateness of the behaviour and the establishment of consequences should be addressed immediately and certainly *before* the student is allowed to continue taking part in the lesson (you may wish to call upon the intervention of senior staff / behaviour support).

Step Four: Seek a resolution

A resolution will depend on the nature of the problem and the students' willingness to concede. Never force a situation. Use your judgement and, if necessary, allow a cooling-off period. At the same time, do not let it slide away unnoticed: you may forget, but your students will not. Whether one student is more at fault than the other, it is often helpful to get both students to apologize for their part in the argument – hence the importance of establishing who said what to who, unless of course it is entirely one-sided. When asking students to apologize, make sure they do a thorough job: have them address each other properly, looking at one another, maybe shake hands, expressing their acceptance of each others apology. Apologies should be related to specific behaviour ('I'm sorry for . . .'). Always praise a student for making a sound apology as it's never an easy thing to do.

12 | Coping with physical aggression

Fighting

Picture the scene. One kid squares up to the other, out of the blue. Giving all the 'come on then' hand gestures. Everything stops. Pens down, eyes turn – they never give *you* this much attention! Before you can fully register what is unfolding, Naseem is standing up raucously, knocking over his desk and chair in a way that signals trouble:

'Yeah. You want some? Come on then . . . come on then. Right here.'

A chorus of students start twittering: 'Yeah . . . there's some beef!' (Don't ask me what it means, perhaps its an east London thing.)

The more sensible ones are shrieking: 'Sir, they're gonna fight – stop them. Sir? Shall I get Mr Sheik?'

You step swiftly towards the trouble zone, stern words leaping from your mouth: 'Boys! Sit down . . .'

But they are deep in the red mist. They don't hear your words. They don't care what you think right now. They're certainly not interested in whatever punishment you can threaten them with. There's a score to settle.

As your words fall on unhearing ears, desks are shoved aside, chairs knocked over. Fists fly and grapple as shirts are pulled, and ties are yanked. It's ugly. And dirty. The front row seats start to chant and jeer. Mob rule.

An unnerving situation, particularly if you are relatively new to the profession.

You cannot always know the ins and outs of your students' relationship dynamics. They have their own battles and triumphs within their youthful community. So how do you anticipate conflict between members of your class when you are not always in the know? Actually, you probably know more than you realize. You may instinctively sense that something is wrong as the kids bundle into the classroom. There is always a precocious child that likes to be on the teacher's side:

> 'Miss – Nick and Billy have had an argument . . . Billy says he's gonna smack Nick's head in . . .'
> 'Thanks Samantha, I'll bear that in mind.'

Other teachers may have information, so keep your ear to the staffroom door. Be aware. If you know where to look, you can see trouble before it gets out of control. If you, yourself, have become aware of an undercurrent of conflict or tension, pass this information on. Imagine a fight has nearly erupted in your lesson. Thanks to your expertise, you have successfully contained it with no further difficulties – is your job completed? Well, yes. Your responsibility for the time being is over, but someone else may have to pick up the pieces later on. Young people, especially those with ESBD, can find it difficult to let go of issues. Grudges can be held for ages. One day Ally smacks Danny in the face. Ally what was that for? He hid my coat. Yes, Ally – but that was two months ago. So? (true story).

Sharing information need not be time-consuming. You could send a brief note to the next teacher (via a very trustworthy student), simply alerting them to the potential conflict between Pupil X and Pupil Y. At breaktime you could bring it to the attention of the tutor(s) or head of year. Perhaps you'll get the: 'Those two? Oh yeah . . . they're always fighting!' reaction, but at least you've acted responsibly – and as a firm believer in what goes around comes around, I believe you'll benefit in the long run! Effective communication and the sharing of information are vital if a school is to succeed in overcoming conflict.

Fights invariably start with verbal altercation. Be proactive and vigilant. Intervene when the first of the spiteful comments emerge, and you may prevent a physical drama. Hesitate, and it could be too late. The longer an individual is allowed to lock into an argument, the less receptive they will be to outside involvement. Interventions need not always be heavy-handed. You hear a phrase containing the words 'your' and 'mum':

> 'Jimmy – come here please . . . you're not in any trouble, I just want to check something out with you.'

Jimmy shuffles over to your desk.

'Wot?'

'I want to make sure that there isn't a problem between you and Daniel – both of you seem quite annoyed with one another. Is there something that we need to sort out?'

'No.'

'Well, I am quite concerned, because I heard some unpleasant comments from both of you. I really don't want either of you to get into any trouble today, because you've had a great week so far. I'm going to give you a choice: either you, me and Daniel sort the problem out now – calmly. *Or* we'll fetch your work and you can come and sit at this desk near me – not because you're in any trouble, but so that no one can wind you up . . .'

'I'll come and sit here, Miss.'

'Good, mature decision Jimmy – I think that deserves a merit.'

When trying to prevent arguments from escalating, your primary aim should be to separate the individuals who are at loggerheads. Whether this requires discreetly asking one of them to speak to you at your desk, or directing a student out of the classroom, you need to ensure that the lines of communication are temporarily severed. If a group of individuals are arguing, aim to remove the main protagonist/the most aggressive. Once you have separated the students you can consider ways of tackling the problem – if they are compliant, you may be able to resolve the issue there and then. If tempers are still too high or the problem is complicated, consider keeping the individuals separated and then revisit the issue later. Do not take a student's word that there is 'no problem' as this is rarely an accurate interpretation of events. Look out for physical signs: a tense jaw, clenched fists, furrowed brow, etc.

If a conflict escalates too quickly to be prevented it is easy to feel overwhelmed and intimidated by the situation. If, like me, you are considerably smaller than the average Year 9, it is likely that your physicality will be lost in the shadow of some angry teenagers. But being small does not mean you cannot project assertiveness and confidence. Use your voice and your physical presence, remain calm and focus on a few key aims:

1   Send for help.
2   Remove the audience.
3   Separate the individuals.
4   Redirect.
5   Calm the atmosphere.
6   Follow-up.

I appreciate that there are differing opinions on how to deal with fighting. Many teachers would prefer to step back, while others will react immediately and directly to the actual fight, pulling individuals off one another. This approach may reduce the risk of students sustaining injuries, which is especially important if you are aware that the aggression is one-sided: there is nothing more disturbing than seeing an innocent individual being hurt. However, it also has its downsides: the main one being that you yourself will be put at risk. (Plus there is a school of thought to suggest that a student getting a fist in their face can be an effective learning curve – especially if they've asked for it!)

For the purposes of this book, I will focus on alternatives to direct handling, as I feel this is a safer approach all round, but you need to make a judgement over what is right for you. Obviously, intervention is a lot easier to manage with younger, smaller students. Personally, I will not get involved unless I know the students well and trust their reactions, and even then, I will use the lightest possible approach. Training in physical restraint is useful (and essential if it is likely that you will need to use it), but it is still difficult to administer in the heat of the moment – and besides, should only ever be a last resort.

Step One: Send for help

This is not a sign of weakness. It is an essential health and safety measure. Even if you are confident that you can contain a fight yourself, additional people will be needed to help smooth the process of resolution, and, if necessary, escort students to senior staff / medical assistance. There is usually a responsible student to hand, one that will intuitively know to go and get help with just a nod from you. In these circumstances, the nearest available staff member should be sought. From experience, I have never known a fellow staff member not oblige. Likewise, I have always prioritized assisting a colleague facing a tough situation over anything else: teamwork is essential when dealing with volatile situations.

Step Two: Remove the audience

Whether you stumble across a fight in the corridor, or it erupts in your own classroom, the situation will always be exacerbated by the presence of other students. You can be certain that any other individuals in the vicinity will automatically turn their attentions to the action. There will be one or two who heroically fling themselves into the arena in a bid to break up the mauling. A few more that will take up defensive stances and may end up joining in with the fight, but at the very least will chant and goad the participants. And there will, of course, be a large crowd of inactive onlookers simply enjoying a spectator sport. Whatever happens, removing the audience can be an effective way of diffusing a fight without having to get involved, as honour, or 'saving face', plays a huge role in youth identity. If there is no one around to admire their left hook, they might not be so inclined to use it.

Focus your attention away from the fight and onto the rest of your students. This is not as easy as it sounds: your natural instincts may tell you to dive right into the action – but remember this has risks. You will need to express yourself loudly and sternly to ensure that your method of communication rises above the noise of the mob. Get the vultures to move on:

> 'Move away – this is not your problem. Don't get involved. You need to sit back down. Right away please.'

If you feel students are at risk – if they are close to the fight or likely to be targeted by an aggressive individual – ensure that they are able to move away from the danger zone. Your aim is to isolate the brawlers, and minimize the involvement of anyone else.

Step Three: Separate the individuals

By the time you have managed to secure some distance between the fighters and their audience the action may have fizzled out, making further intervention less risky. If they are still at it full-throttle, and you do not feel comfortable about intervening, wait for your backup. If you are confident about getting involved, do so, but with the minimum force possible: be cautious, not heroic. Always turn your own face away from the action, to avoid misfired punches. Bring your arm between the brawlers, or alternatively, grip one of the individual's shoulders and direct them away.

Physical interventions of this kind are always more successful when you have additional assistance. It is important to have someone taking responsibility for each individual so they can both be led away from each other. It is difficult to secure the safety of your student when their enemy is still free to attack them. A cautionary tale: a student was fighting in class and his support worker intervened and held the student back by his arm, thus leading him away from the fight. His assailant smacked him thrice in the face. The student could not defend himself as his arm was being held!

In the heat of tension it is very easy for concerns to become confused and cluttered. If a person is in a state of arousal, in other words, anticipating aggressive action, they will be under stress. If they are under stress, they will probably express themselves in a stressed-out way. You may get a rather rude response as you try to intervene. You may not want this, but do not be bothered by it just yet. Deal with the primary concern (deflecting physical conflict) and worry about the 'Don't you speak to me like that' details later.

Step Four: Redirect

As soon as you have managed to separate the fighters, they will need to be directed away from one another, out of each other's sight-line, and to a quiet area where they can regain composure. Ideally, there will be an adult available to see to each student. If not, decide who of the fighters is the most volatile and deal with them first. There is often a group of sympathetic classmates that will make a fuss of the other individual until you are ready to deal with them; alternatively, they could be sent to the office or to another classroom.

The most effective way to calm an angry person is to be very calm yourself. This is not the time to shout, accuse or be stroppy. Speak to the student in an even, firm tone of voice. If you feel you need to contain them physically, be as unintrusive as possible, for instance, a reassuring hand on their shoulder or arm. Encourage them to calm down – nothing else needs to be discussed until they are calm. If they struggle and yell at you to leave them alone, calmly and clearly re-assure them that you will be happy to leave them alone, as soon as you can see that they are calm and not about to put themselves in any more danger. As soon as you sense they are getting control of themselves again – the time this takes will vary considerably from student to student – praise and encourage them.

When you want an agitated pupil to follow specific directions (in any situation, not just fighting), just give them those directions and little else – try not to confuse anxious thought processes. I can recall an alarming incident with a very angry Year 7 student threatening to throw himself off the second-floor balcony while teetering on the railings above the school foyer. I could not touch him, partly because I feared a movement towards him would entice him into actually jumping. I had to rely on verbal reasoning:

> 'I would like you to climb down – I can see that you are very upset . . . I want to help you . . . I need you to climb down and I can help you to sort your problem out.'

Empathizing and identifying with a student, expressing a wish to listen and help, are valuable verbal methods of reassuring a person and negotiating the preferred outcome. Of course, you may feel angry with the child: for their immaturity, or the way they have disrupted your lesson, for the fact that they are forever causing problems – but your priority is to get them as far from an angry state of mind as possible, minimizing the chances of further harm.

When the student is calm, and only when *you* are certain of this (do not take the student's word for it), it is time to start unravelling the problem. Let the student talk before making accusations. Establish their perception of how the fight started, and who did what:

> 'Okay Gary, I can see you're much calmer now and that's really helpful. I need you to tell me exactly what happened?'
> 'Daniel called my mum a slag.'
> 'Right. When was this?'
> 'In the lesson. He's a fat prick!'
> 'Okay . . . Okay. I know you're very annoyed with him, but saying that sort of thing is not going to help you right now. We need to sort this out . . .'
> 'I'm not sorting anything out with him.'
> 'But you do need to sort things out with me – and you may have to sort things out with other staff members as well, because fighting is very serious. So what happened: in your own words, but be as honest as you can . . .'
> 'I was just reading my book, and he leaned over and whispered right in my ear that his brothers and his mates are gonna do me in after school . . . and then he said that my mum's a slag.'
> 'That's not very nice. So how did you react to that?'
> 'Nuffink. I didn't do nuffink. I told him to leave me alone.'

'Are you sure? You see, I'm going to have to speak to him and find out his version of events, so if you tell me the truth now, it will really help you . . . did you say anything back to him?'

'I said his brother was a moron.'

'Right – not a very kind thing to say, but I'm sure you know that. Well thank you for being honest. It seems to me that both of you have said some things to wind each other up. Would you agree?'

'Yeah . . . but he started it.'

'Well, we obviously need to get to the bottom of what he and his brothers are planning – but we also need to decide what will happen to you two for the rest of the day. You both know that I don't have fighting in my classroom, and I don't have people saying unkind things to one another, so there will have to be consequences for that behaviour. I understand that you were both angry with each other, but there are much better ways to deal with this than fighting, and you're both going to have to work on that. Otherwise, it spoils things for you, it's not fair on the rest of the class, and it's not fair me because I like teaching you, not breaking up your fights!'

'Yes Miss.'

'So how can you put things right with me?'

'Sorry for fighting Miss.'

'Thank you. Now, I need you to go to Miss Clark's class for the rest of the lesson while I speak to Daniel and the rest of the class. The reason I'm asking *you* to move is because I know you'll be very sensible about it. When the lesson is finished, I want to speak to you and Daniel together, so we can come to some agreement about how you two are going to get on with the rest of the day, and make up for the problems that your fighting has caused. If you do that in a grown-up way, then I won't have to send you to the head of year, will I?'

Step Five: Calm the atmosphere

When the situation has stabilized, you will need to return your attention to the rest of the class. Allow time for the air to settle before launching back into work. Briefly acknowledge what has happened, and explain that the students are being dealt with. After such an event, other students in the class may be feeling distressed, worried, excited or hyper. There will probably be a lot of nervous chatter and gossip spreading through the room. Some students may feel the need to vocalize their opinions about who was right/who was wrong/who got the best punch in. This is only natural. You could allow them 5 minutes to air their views and debrief, or alternatively, invite them to discuss their version of events after class – they may have some useful insight into the background of the conflict.

Encourage the class to settle down, and praise any individuals, or maybe the whole class, for their maturity/not getting involved/ behaving sensibly. Return to work, but do not expect the most productive session ever – consider modifying the task in order to accommodate fractured nerves. Perhaps students would benefit from a quiet calming activity like designing a poster or silent reading. Or perhaps a group game, which can reunite the solidarity of the class: hangman, or for younger students, a story.

Step Six: Follow-up

The ease with which a volatile situation, such as a fight, can be managed depends upon the availability of other adults to help out. If others can take the matter into their hands, it decreases the burden on you and frees you to focus on teaching and working with the whole class. However, you should always endeavour to be involved in the process of following up the problem. It is always tempting to step back when an issue has been taken out of your hands and is in the lap of senior managers. But do not step back entirely. Support those dealing with the matter, provide what information and assistance you can, and do not accept the students back into your class until you are confident that the matter has been adequately addressed.

See things through. It enhances your status if students see that you are in tune with what is going on, that you communicate with the 'big guns', that you all stick together! After a serious incident, it is important to have a meeting between yourself, the students and other staff members involved in dealing with it (for example, senior managers). Expect an apology from the students, with evidence that they have made amends to one another and are receiving appropriate consequences for their actions (this will depend on the gravity of the incident).

Never feel that you have to just tolerate things. If you are taking the responsibility of doing everything you can to contain and improve classroom behaviour, you should be able to expect that if problems occur, other staff will support you and ensure that your limits are respected. A student should never be allowed to casually return to a class that they have severely disrupted, and this includes returning after a period of exclusion. It undermines your position and can contribute to stress. If students do not see that they are accountable to you, and that you do not accept inappropriate behaviour, they are less likely to respect your instructions in the future. A reintegration discussion should be held where full attention can be given from all parties and the outcome is satisfactory.

The fact is, dealing with fights or incidents of physical misconduct takes time and skill to sort out effectively. Many teachers have the skill, but they do not have the time. It is important, therefore, that the chances of this behaviour occurring are minimized, and so the first level of action should be preventative: recognizing the symptoms of a possible fight, knowing how to address and diffuse the issues, sharing information and knowing you have support around you.

Physical assault

Staff members being assaulted by their students – alarming, but it does happen. Fortunately it is not a frequent occurrence, but understandably, it is an emotive subject that is a large cause for concern. Such incidents are entirely unacceptable. It is vital, however, that they are not devoured by sensationalism, but are understood and addressed in ways that are rational and productive.

If you are concerned about the risk of assault against yourself, focus on preventative measures:

◆ Know your students and identify triggers (find out what their needs are and endeavour to understand these and try to build positive links with them).
◆ Intervene early (address problems as soon as possible at the lowest level possible).
◆ Use techniques to de-escalate (speak calmly, be firm but polite, offer a way out, avoid rising to conflict, give the individual space).
◆ Focus on respect (give it, and you will be more likely to receive it).

My experience of working with ESBD students of all ages suggests that younger students are actually more likely to get physical with you. If they become angry or upset this is how they may choose to express themselves – perhaps compensating for limited skills of verbal reasoning. They lash out or have tantrums, whereas an older child might resort to verbal abuse, perhaps having developed a more 'mature' level of self-restraint. Violence is never something that should be tolerated, but it is always worth keeping in the back of your mind that if a young child hits, kicks or pushes you, the chances are they are not intending to hurt you, but are trying – inappropriately and inefficiently – to make their point. Do not take it personally.

If you are the victim of an unpleasant classroom assault, this needs to be addressed immediately. You may be stunned, shocked and you might be hurt. No one will think less of you if your first instinct is to leave the room. Seek the nearest staff member for some assistance – they can ensure that the rest of your class will be attended to, and that senior staff will be alerted. If you feel able to retain your composure in front of the class, do so, but your assailant will need to be removed and dealt with (if they have not already run away!). There is no need to try to gloss over such a serious matter: your students will probably be as horrified as you are.

Seek support and allow yourself some time to get your head together, but make sure you write out an incident report as close to the event as possible. If you are injured you will need to have this documented. Give yourself a break and a thorough chance to recover before contemplating going back to class. You may even feel the need to take the rest of the day off. It is important that you listen to your instincts, and do not feel guilty about neglecting your duties. Stress and its effects need to be respected.

Many would argue that assault on a teacher should be a last-chance event for a student in mainstream education, resulting in permanent exclusion (although special needs schools have different limitations – believe me – the amount of times I've been headbutted, pinched, scratched, kicked, spat at . . .). If permanent exclusion is the result, you will avoid having to face that individual again. However, permanent exclusion, for various reasons, is not always the chosen option. If this is the case, you will have to come to terms with the fact that you will be sharing a building, if not a classroom, with your assailant – although they should at least receive a fixed-term (temporary) exclusion.

Being placed in this situation may be extremely difficult. You need to judge for yourself whether you feel it is reasonable or not. You will certainly find supporters if you wish to resist the possibility of having further interactions with a student that has assaulted you. Unions are a key source of information, guidance and support. Other colleagues may also back you up.

It is possible, however, to repair fractured nerves and damaged student–teacher relationships. I know this, because it is an integral part of the process of working in an ESBD school: we have to forgive and move on. If students are not given second chances in this kind of specialist environment, they run out of options altogether. Though less probable, forgiveness can have its place in mainstream settings too. My first real incident of ESBD behaviour occurred while I was a very naive NQT. A difficult Year 8 student suddenly lost his temper with another child, and began brandishing a chair at him, before telling everyone to 'f**k off!' and running out of the room. Being so inexperienced, I found the whole situation too much to bear, and failed to keep the tears from watering my eyes; thus was kindly relieved of my duties by my head of department. I spent the next few days shuddering at the thought of meeting this particular student again, and cursing myself for the fact that I had been so 'weak'. Until he appeared at my classroom door one lunchtime:

> 'Miss! I heard that you cried. I didn't never want to make you cry. I like you Miss. All the class are really angry with me – can I be forgiven?'

And from that moment on, he became one of my most committed, charming and helpful students.

Students who self-harm

Self-harm involves the deliberate attempt to physically injure oneself, and can include cutting, burning, biting, scalding, head-banging, poisoning or pulling out hair. There is growing concern about the number of teenagers who engage in this distressing behaviour, and I receive ongoing inquiries from teachers who are concerned about students in their classes.

It is often a very secretive behaviour (injuries can be performed in private and covered by clothing), therefore not always easy to identify. And although it is commonly assumed that such dramatic action is a 'cry for help', or a means of seeking attention, many self-harmers argue that it is, in fact, a way of 'coping'. The extreme intensity of the harm they do to themselves brings relief. Risk factors include:

◆ Depression or obsessive compulsive disorder.
◆ Eating disorders.
◆ Low self-esteem and self-worth.

◆ Experience of physical, emotional or sexual abuse.
◆ Internal anger.
◆ Bullying.

If you are concerned about self-harmers in your class, first find out if your school has a policy on what to do. If a student confides in you about the issue, you cannot and should not promise confidentiality, so it's important to know who you can turn to for further advice and support. In every case, a judgement needs to be made, ensuring that the trust of the young person isn't unnecessarily damaged, but that the right measures are taken to ensure their personal welfare.

Young people who self-harm may require the support of specialists, such as counsellors and other therapeutic and/or medical services. Providing this level of intervention is not your responsibility, but you can still play a valuable role. If a student approaches you on the matter, they obviously see you as someone positive and supportive. Communication is important. Let them know that you are available, whenever possible, if they want to talk. It may be helpful to reassure them that self-harm is common – that it's nothing to be ashamed of and that they're not alone, and to offer general advice on anger management, such as breathing techniques, distraction, vigorous exercise, or writing down thoughts and feelings.

Encourage students who self-harm to make a list of people they can turn to in times of desperation. This could include yourself, friends, family, other teachers or support lines such as Childline or the Samaritans. It is also important to reiterate the need for good personal care and hygiene, and perhaps direct them towards basic first-aid courses. Self-harmers don't necessarily have a death-wish, so if they are going to do it to themselves, they will be better off knowing basic procedures such as cleaning wounds with antiseptic, not re-using blades, and contacting emergency services for serious injuries.

Gang culture and weapons in school

Concerns about gang culture and weapons have been growing over recent years, and rarely a day goes by when there isn't some sort of youth violence news story hitting the headlines. The issue, and fears about the issue, cause tension and anxiety for staff and students alike. It's not a pleasant thing to acknowledge, but if it's happening, the worst thing a school/community can do is deny its presence.

A number of measures can be taken to minimize and manage the problem, such as local schools staggering start and finish times (to avoid clashes between rival gangs), scanning machines to detect and prevent weapons being carried into the school building, CCTV, high security fencing, and even on-site police. A strong policy is imperative, with clear, firm consequences for any breach of conduct. Schools need to be established as neutral ground – that means no tolerance of weapons, violence, harassment, illegal activity (drugs, theft, etc.), or gang-related clothing, symbols and gestures.

The issue, of course, runs deeper than school policy. The key question is *why* are young people getting involved in gangs/carrying weapons? This is society's problem, and not just the responsibility of individual schools. Research has pointed to a number of causes:

◆ Lack of positive role models.
◆ Glamorization of gangs and drugs.
◆ Absence of father in the home.
◆ Too much freedom (British youth are thought to spend less time in the company of adults than anywhere else in Europe – so where/with whom are they forming their value systems?).
◆ Wanting a sense of 'belonging'.
◆ Wanting protection.

In terms of helping to tackle the origins of the problem, you and your school can play a vital role in educating and working to improve your students' communication skills, self-esteem, sense of identity, and sense of moral code and responsibility. Personal, health, social, and citizenship education should be high on any schools' agenda, as should the provision of opportunities to engage in positive group activity (e.g. sport, drama, music, outdoor pursuits, community work).

If you, as an individual, are faced with the reality of a dangerous gang/weapon-related situation, such as students threatening one another or suspecting a weapon, unless you have been fully trained, have assessed the risk to yourself, and are willing, you do *not* have to physically intervene/carry out a search. In any case, two adults should be present, for both your safety and the students. Your number one priority, therefore, is to get back-up.

13 | Coping with the pressure

This section considers the issue of how challenging behaviour can affect you and your stress levels, and what you can do to help yourself. Dealing with difficult students can be highly stressful – particularly if the problems seem relentless or personally aimed at you. The number one rule, of course, is to never, EVER take things personally – even if it seems like they are trying to wind you up/deliberately disrupt your lesson/insult you/constantly get the better of you.

That said, we are all human and we all have a breaking point. Most teachers, experienced or otherwise, will have a story about the time they were pushed to their limits and reacted in an emotional way; perhaps bursting into tears or losing their temper. Every now and again, it happens. If it's happening on a regular basis, however, there is a problem.

First, it's an unreasonable amount of unpleasantness to be putting up with – and certainly not the reason you took up a career in teaching. Abuse is a strong word, but many teachers feel that this is what they are subjected to, sometimes daily. The constant battle against it can be demoralizing and tiresome. Poor behaviour is frequently cited as the number one reason for teachers leaving the profession.

Second, if the behaviour of the students gets to you, you may be less resilient when it comes to dealing with the next class or the next situation. Many teachers also have stories about times when they've taken out their backlog of stress on otherwise innocent class groups or students. This can lead to problems with the way in which students regard you: do they find you trustworthy, reasonable and reassuring? Or do they think you're erratic, unpredictable and unfair?

Third, if some students see that their antics are having a negative effect on you this may simply encourage them. Unfortunately you can't rely on them to feel remorseful, or to know when they've crossed the line, especially when crossing the line is something they are actively trying to do. Teacher baiting isn't nice, but then there are a lot of misguided, emotionally mixed-up characters out there.

The key to salvation is learning how to react to the 'abuse' from a place of professional skill rather than from emotion, separating personal feelings and frustrations from the literal practice of managing behaviour. If you can master this, your teaching career will be far less stressful, no matter how difficult the students are, and it will enhance your reputation as a teacher who doesn't tolerate foolery and will not be fazed; which in turn, will make your life easier – students will know to respect and not to mess. So how do you achieve this? Here are some suggestions.

School support systems

Although teaching can sometimes feel like a solitary profession, it is important to remember that there are others like you just down the corridor. You're not alone, and when the pressure is on, there are people who can support you in a number of ways. Maybe the teacher next door can 'babysit' one of your disruptive students for the rest of the lesson, giving you and the class some breathing room (you can return the favour another time). Perhaps you and your department colleagues can form a detention cooperative – taking turns to run them on alternate nights. Maybe you just need to off-load your stress about a terrible lesson in the staffroom, to colleagues who AREN'T going to smile smugly and undermine you.

Schools will generally have a range of support systems to help staff tackle challenging behaviour. Some of these will be formal, for example, behaviour policies, 'on-call' systems, referral systems, reward and consequence schemes, whole-school rules. Others will be informal (although no less important), for example, communication, consistency and cooperation amongst staff.

The reason why informal support matters is because formal systems of dealing with behaviour generally rely on it. Unless staff are committed to the policy, principles and structures in place, everything can unravel. This counts at all levels of seniority, from the maverick NQT who decides that sticking to the school uniform rule is too much like hard work, to the 'on-call' senior manager who can never be found during the crisis.

Whatever the formal systems and policies are, they need to be workable. Staff are more likely to embrace policy when they feel that it will be achievable and effective; in order to ensure relevance, there is a need for these things to be regularly reviewed and refined, in consultation with those using them. It all comes back to communication.

Coping under pressure

Facing a rowdy group, dealing with a fight, or perhaps being on the receiving end of a student's attempts to insult or intimidate you – these are highly stressful situations. Hopefully they are infrequent occurrences in your lessons, but being mentally prepared to cope with them is an important aspect of successfully dealing with challenging behaviour. Remaining calm and in control will benefit you and your students, and help to resolve the situation.

The above are extreme examples that anyone would find difficult, but be aware of your own personal stressors. Little things can accumulate over time and impact on your ability to cope. Maybe it's frustration about constant low-level disruption, anxiety about Ofsted, the mountain of paperwork, or personal stress.

Everyone feels frustration, stress and anger – they are understandable responses to difficult situations. The key is in how they are expressed. In many ways, successful management of student behaviour is about learning to manage your own reactions and responses to it. Running out of patience, losing your temper and having a go at a student is NOT a behaviour management strategy – it is a knee-jerk emotional reaction. Here are some alternative suggestions to help you keep your cool:

◆ Think business-like, neutral and matter-of-fact. Keep your comments bland and to the point: 'We don't talk to people like that, thank you.'
◆ If students try to provoke you, shrug and look bemused, as though their behaviour is highly strange but definitely not upsetting to you.
◆ Make a point of giving your attention to students who *are* getting on with the lesson.
◆ Count to ten and exhale slowly (slowing your breath can be very calming).
◆ Remind yourself it's just a job/it's not personal, the students have their own problems/there's a cold pint waiting for you at the end of the day!
◆ Defer your response: 'I'll speak to you at the end of class.'
◆ Give students take-up time, i.e. give them an instruction then walk away. Avoid getting entangled.

Assertiveness

Anxiety goes hand in hand with stress. Unless you feel confident and self-assured the classroom can be a scary place – especially if you are expecting students to mess about and challenge your authority. And if they pick up on your nerves, they may be tempted to take advantage of them. Many teachers argue that, even if it's not possible to truly *feel* bold and at ease (we all have our 'off' days) it is essential to at least *project* that image. In other words, fake it! Think of your teaching as a performance – perhaps a few sessions at drama school should be part of the teacher training curriculum. Walk into that room like it's your castle.

Experience makes it easier. But of course, the only way to gain experience is through simply getting on with it. My advice to new teachers is not to be put off by the struggles; not to feel defeated when things go wrong or mistakes are made – treat everything as a learning opportunity. In two years' time you'll look back and see how far you've come.

It also helps to watch what other teachers do – how they present themselves and how they communicate. Observe their body language, the projection and tone of their voice, and the type of words/phrases they use. Simple things can make a difference, such as saying 'Thank you' instead of 'Please', or phrasing requests as statements rather than questions: 'You need to sit down thank you', is more emphatic than, 'Can you all sit down now please?' which begs a cheeky response: yes, I *could* sit down . . . but I'm not going to!

Assertiveness is NOT about shouting, dominating or 'bullying' students into behaving. It's about knowing what you want and sticking up for it. A useful starting point is to work out what your teaching values are and what you want to achieve with your students. If you're clear in your own mind about your intentions, it is easier to convey them to other people.

Where to get help

If negative stress has got the better of you and you've reached the stage where the mere thought of certain classes or students brings you out in a cold sweat, it is important to get support. A stressed-out teacher is unlikely to be an effective teacher, and is far more likely to say or do something they regret when dealing with confrontation and challenging behaviour. Signs to look out for include:

- General feelings of anxiety (not necessarily school-related)
- Loss/increased appetite
- Disrupted sleep
- Stomach upsets
- Frequent illness (stress suppresses the immune system)
- Feelings of exhaustion
- Mood swings and string emotions (tearful, short-tempered, aggressive, etc.)
- Physical symptoms (weight loss/gain, hair loss, skin problems, twitches, headaches, nausea, jaw tension)
- Feelings of panic or hysteria
- Increased alcohol/smoking
- Intense feelings of dread about going to school
- Negative self-image and feelings of failure
- Inability to wind down and relax, even at weekends.

Early recognition and intervention are essential. Stress is accumulative and the longer it continues, the deeper the damage. At its worst stress can be highly debilitating and may require a lengthy recovery period. There is no shame; it is something that can happen to anyone, at any level – from headteachers to newly qualifieds.

Fortunately, there are things you can do to protect yourself. Think practical. First, establish a support network: people you can talk to. Your network could involve friends and family (who can remind you of the good things in life), trusted colleagues (who can empathize and relate to your experiences) and line managers (who, if necessary, can take practical measures to reassure you, reduce your workload or alleviate pressure). You may also want to take advice from your union, your GP or your local occupational health services.

Second, learn to set clear boundaries for yourself. Prioritize what needs to be done; don't sweat about the non-essential or less important things. Take your breaks. Delegate tasks to others (colleagues/classroom assistants/sensible students). Put time-limits on paperwork and restrict the amount of work you take home. Eat well, stay hydrated and get regular exercise (even if you don't feel like it, physical activity is a great way to reduce tension and releases feel-good endorphins).

Last, set realistic expectations of yourself. Recognize that you can't do everything and that you can't (and don't *need* to) be perfect. This doesn't mean you are a failure – it just means you are normal!

14 | Common questions answered

This chapter examines some of the common behaviour management scenarios that occur in schools. They are real, day-to-day concerns posed by real teachers, so hopefully there is something that everyone can relate to. The solutions provide practical, relevant advice intended to make life in the classroom easier.

QUESTION: How do I deal with students who dislike/are disengaged with the subject I teach?

SCENARIO: I teach Modern Foreign Languages in a secondary school, and specialize in German. I have ongoing battles with my students about why they need to be learning German. They constantly argue that there's no point, they're never going to use it – I'm beginning to wonder whether it's worth it. Every lesson, it takes me ages to get them settled and working.

SOLUTION: Rule number one, don't ever let the attitude of a group of teenagers make you feel despondent about the subject you have chosen to study and now teach – you picked it for a reason, therefore you must see something valuable and enjoyable in it. If you stop caring about it, your students most certainly will. If, on the other hand, you can adopt an attitude of passion for your subject this can have the opposite effect. Think of the infectious enthusiasm of television presenters, such as Tony Robinson, who has brought history and archaeology programmes to the attention of the nation. Even if you feel slightly ridiculous doing it, go for it! If you're buzzing with energy about your lessons, this should rub off on the students.

Establish and retain high expectations. Don't allow standards to slip, just because motivation is lacking – it's a downward spiral. For example, if students are half-hearted about homework, get a system. Try checking that homework has been done during the lesson, before collecting it in. Keep a clear record of who hasn't produced. Two late homeworks means a consequence, such as detention/phone-call home.

In terms of class work, a number of approaches can help:

◆ Get students on-task as soon as they enter the room, minimizing the opportunity for social chat. Something simple and engaging, such as 'Write two sentences on whether you agree with . . .'. This could be the starting point for further discussion and debate.

◆ Introduce a competitive element, working in teams or as individuals, perhaps with small prizes. External motivators such as this, although they are no replacement for genuine effort, can help kick-start a disengaged class.

◆ Break tasks into smaller chunks and mix up different activities, so that there is variety within the lesson. Keep the pace going. Even the most interesting of subjects can be dull if they are delivered in a dry, non-interactive way.

◆ Try to link material to what they know already, or what is relevant to their world. Tasks can easily be adapted to reflect current issues and interests, such as youth crime, celebrity culture or sport, which will make them more attractive.

QUESTION: How do I manage to remain calm and 'neutral' when my students are deliberately trying to press my buttons?

SCENARIO: I feel like I'm being 'picked-on' by a group of Year 9 girls. Their behaviour includes sniggering and whispering about me, and mimicking me during lessons. They do it when I'm trying to reprimand other students, and it really undermines my confidence. I feel angry and frustrated. It's got to the point where I get wound up and start stressing and shouting, but unfortunately, this just makes them worse.

SOLUTION: First, don't suffer in silence. Talk to other teachers or your head of department – who can bolster you and step in as back-up if necessary. The chances are you're not the only one to be a victim of this behaviour and knowing this can give you some comfort. It's important not to ignore teacher 'baiting' or bullying – it is unacceptable and this message needs to be made clear. That said, don't allow it to get the better of you. Sometimes it's a matter of reminding yourself about all the good things you've got in your life, and dismissing student–teacher baiting as jealousy, insecurity or bitterness.

The key is to address the matter without bringing personal emotions into it. Finding another outlet for upset and frustration is helpful – if you manage to control/hide your emotions in front of the students, it is perfectly understandable that you will still experience them. It's all about *where* you experience them (i.e. not in front of the students), because if they think they're hitting the target, like any bully, they will persist.

Arm yourself with a selection of responses, and practise getting into the mindset you want to have in front of the bullies. Being prepared will help you to react from skill rather than from knee-jerk emotion. Some suggestions:

◆ The firm but detached approach: 'We don't talk to people like that in here, thank you' followed by a warning, 'We have a rule about respect. If you choose to continue, you realize it will lead to a detention/note home/etc.'. There is no need to linger on this – be glib and matter-of-fact then go and give your attention to other students. You've made your point, given them a clear warning, demonstrated that you're not personally bothered by their antics – rules and consequences will take care of the rest.

◆ The diversion approach: instead of focusing on yourself, emphasize to the students that their behaviour is distracting your attention from the rest of the class/wasting valuable time/etc. This is effective if there are other students in the class who want to work and will share your annoyance – peer pressure. Raising the matter with parents can also help.

◆ The shocked approach: 'You think this is funny? Perhaps you'd like to go and laugh about it with your head of year? Which can be arranged . . . right now if you like?' Effective but it requires a confident, no-nonsense delivery.

◆ The deferred approach: if in any doubt, take a few relaxing breaths, give a withering look of boredom, and when they've finished (realizing they haven't gained the desired response – your lack of it is a powerful message, i.e. you aren't bothered, you've heard it all before) calmly take the appropriate procedures according to your behaviour policy (e.g. student withdrawal, detention, etc.)

◆ The dismissive approach: a quiet 'okay' or 'fine' to each comment, followed by a quick refocus on class work, will flatten their efforts. 'Your teaching is crap . . .' 'Okay . . . so let's see where we've got to then . . .', 'My brother hates you . . .' 'Fine . . . now, have you managed to finish the questions or would you like some help?'

◆ The one-to-one approach: if you can convey confidence and rationale, a low-key chat about the problem (if it's a group, focus on the ring-leader), away from other students, can be all that is needed to eliminate the behaviour. Explain that it is unfair and that it has to stop – present yourself as friendly, reasonable and, dare I say it, keen to build a more positive relationship, and you may well see a transformation!

QUESTION: How do I manage the challenge of dealing with a few difficult students while not neglecting the rest of the class?

SCENARIO: I have a mixed-ability Year 5 class. There are 31 students and some days I feel like I'm letting them all down. Generally they are a nice group, but there are a couple of individuals who have challenging behaviour. I get no additional support for having them, and they demand a lot of my time. It just isn't fair on the rest of the class.

SOLUTION: For low-level behaviour, it's important to establish a number of low-level strategies that can curb the problems of the few without taking up too much of your time and attention. If you become adept at this, you will be able to maintain your focus on whole class teaching. Some suggestions include:

◆ The 'look': using a stern face and holding eye-contact can often be enough to show students that you are on to them.
◆ Moving towards the problem: close physical presence has the same effect as the 'look', and doesn't necessarily require you to break your teaching flow.
◆ Making a note of names: as long as students see you do this, know what it means (a first warning), and why they're being included, you don't need to say anything else.
◆ Positive focus on students doing the right things: 'Thank you to the students on the big table, who are showing me that they are ready to listen' – demonstrate/remind students of what you want, rather than what you don't want, and remember to praise the target students as soon as they comply.

A word of warning however – these simple strategies are effective but they take time to bed down. Initially, you may have to work hard at getting them to have an impact. If students aren't responsive at first, you'll need to have back up – a clear, consistent system of warnings and consequences (as described in other chapters), to show students that you mean what you say you do. Otherwise a withering look may simply be just that.

If you are under pressure, it may be tempting to ignore a lot of low-level activity. Tactical ignoring (i.e. letting them know that you know what they're doing, but aren't prepared to waste time on it) can be powerful, but simply letting things go or hoping that they'll go away of their own accord is dangerous. Low-level behaviour, if left unaddressed, can quickly escalate to more extreme disruption, making it harder for you to regain control.

For more extreme disruption, the same system of warnings/consequences applies, although you may need to give up more of your attention in order to tackle the matter fully. With highly disruptive individuals (problems tend to come from the same few), a two-pronged approach is helpful. On the one hand, be strong and swift. If the behaviour isn't going away after the first two warnings, use time-out or student withdrawal (hoping your school has a system in place) – don't try to teach through the disruption. Get the student out of the way, and be clear that unless they are prepared to respect the classroom rules, like everyone else, then there will always be consequences.

It's better to break off and tackle the issue fully than try to grin and bear it. Apologizing to other students can help to keep them in your 'fold': 'I'm sorry that someone in the class is *choosing* to disrupt *your* lesson . . . I'll be with you as soon as I can . . . and thank you for being so sensible.' In consultation with students, they all said they would prefer teachers to stop and deal with troublemakers than to let them carry on disturbing the class.

The second mode of attack – and this is the important bit – is to work extremely hard, in and around the classroom, to build a rapport with the disruptive individuals themselves. If you are having to withdraw them from class on a frequent basis, you need to make it clear that it's the behaviour you are rejecting and not the student. Otherwise, these individuals become increasingly demoralized and isolated from the world of the classroom and the problems don't go away.

QUESTION: How do I deal with colleagues who don't support or back me up?

SCENARIO: I work with a teaching assistant who has a very strong personality. She has a lot of experience but she also has very set ideas about how the students should be dealt with. She says or does things that undermine what I'm trying to do, and sometimes it seems like she's trying to work against me. The inconsistency causes problems and confusion with the class.

SOLUTION: Teaching assistants can make an invaluable contribution to the management of classroom behaviour, but if there is a lack of unity within the team, it can make things a whole lot worse. The same applies to working with managers and other teachers. If we don't present a united front to students, we become vulnerable.

Sometimes effective working relationships fall naturally into place, but if they don't, there are things that can be done to improve them. First, it's important to identify where things are going wrong. It might be something that is easily solved, for instance, a lack of communication. If discussion, reflection and sharing information are lost within the busy day, try scheduling a fixed time, maybe once at the start/end of the week, or shorter daily meetings. Yes it requires effort, but communication should always be a priority.

Teamwork can be enhanced and nurtured by the following suggestions:

◆ Encourage 'open' communication. Don't allow things to fester. Both you and your colleagues should feel able to raise issues without fearing the reaction – this breeds trust and respect. Being open is about being true to your principles but having a willingness to listen to others. It's about honesty, but also flexibility.

◆ Give regular feedback. If someone does something well, tell them. Use praise to encourage and steer people in the right direction. But don't be afraid to raise concerns. Lack of honest appraisal can lull people into a false sense of security. If you're worried about being critical, make it a two-way process. Give staff the opportunity to tell you the things they do/don't agree with about the way you work – it may help clear the air.

◆ Make sure *you* are clear about what you want to achieve with your students – if you don't have aims of your own or fail to provide clear leadership, others are more likely to step in and try to take control.

◆ That said, balance your own vision with making staff feel valued by asking for their advice/opinion. Recognize that they may know more about some of the students than you do. Try not to assume that you always know best.

◆ Identify strengths (e.g. artistic skills, organizational skills, caring nature, sense of humour, rapport with difficult students) and encourage staff to make use of them. Encourage staff to seek quality training to develop their skills.

QUESTION: How do I manage my students' preoccupation with their social lives?

SCENARIO: I am in my sixth year of teaching and I find that some of my students have no idea what the classroom is for. They come in so casually, chatting, flirting, talking about their personal lives, and acting as if the lesson is just another extension of their breaktime. Once I've got them into the work, they're still easily distracted, and it's a constant challenge to keep them focused on the learning. They don't seem to take their education seriously.

SOLUTION: Getting students into the right frame of mind as soon as they enter the classroom is vital. The boundary between personal time and teaching time needs to be firmly established – otherwise, what are you being paid for?

First, a class discussion may help. Their social distraction might not be intentional. The reasons why students disengage with education are many and varied, and are not always the fault of the students themselves. Are they bored? Do they lack encouragement from their parents/their wider community? Do they lack confidence in learning? Generating positive discussion around this topic can help you to understand each other's positions and challenge negative expectations. It also gives you scope to agree on some ground rules.

Make it clear to students that social conversation needs to end as the lesson begins. This can be aided in a number of ways:

◆ Silent entry into the classroom. A no-talking policy eliminates the issue of social chat, but can be hard to enforce – decide what's appropriate for your class.

◆ Allowing for 'controlled' chat time. This is a half-way house: five minutes of chat at the start, to get it out of their systems, while they are settling/getting their books out/etc. As soon as the alarm goes, chat stops.

◆ Greeting students as they come through the door. This allows you to field any big issues. Have particularly excitable students remain outside until the majority of the class are settled.

◆ Offering a reward for maintaining focus and attention, e.g. five minutes of free chat at the end of the lesson, or listening to a piece of music.

◆ Managing the seating plan. This may not be popular, but will allow you to separate chatty pairs and groups. Students can always 'earn' back the right to sit with their friends by showing how sensible they can be.

◆ Communication with parents can help. Most parents would be concerned to know that their child isn't taking their schoolwork seriously.

QUESTION: How do I deal with the student whom nothing seems to work on?

SCENARIO: One of the students at my school is really badly behaved and disrespectful. All the teachers are struggling with him and he doesn't seem to be concerned with any of the sanctions put on him. He acts like he couldn't care less, has no respect for authority, and even the headteacher can't control him a lot of the time.

SOLUTION: It takes serious commitment to support the education of students such as the one described, but they are familiar characters in schools up and down the country. For various reasons these individuals have become chronically disaffected and disengaged with the school experience. It is highly likely that they have grown accustomed to being on the wrong side of the school 'law' and that's where they see themselves – always in trouble, feared/disliked/unwanted by staff. With such a negative self-view, why would they be bothered about sanctions?

As with all behavioural issues, developing an empathic understanding of why the student is doing what they do will help you to cope and deal with it more effectively. Try to see school through their eyes and consider what their underlying motivations might be: Power? Attention?

With individuals like this, there is no point in fighting for authority or trying to win the battle of power – if they are beyond caring about the consequences of their actions, it's likely that they'll be ready to push it further than you will. It's also possible that they are looking for some kind of confrontation (to fulfil their own world view that they are 'trouble') – rising to it will simply fuel this negative spiral.

Work on that all-important rapport. Challenge the student's negative view of teachers and classrooms by welcoming them into your environment. Notice little details: they've sat quietly for two minutes or they've arrived at the lesson on time. Praise every small step in the right direction and start filling their bank of positive experiences. But at the same time, don't protect them from your rules and expectations. Remind them that they are making a choice. If they make a bad one there will be consequences.

No, they may not be bothered by these consequences, but the thing they will be bothered by, if you've built a relationship with them, is your opinion. That's what makes the difference: the sense that somebody *cares*. Instead of anger and annoyance if they misbehave, try expressing regret and disappointment. Keep reminding them that, despite what they may do or think, you have faith in their potential. Be the teacher that they'll remember for all the right reasons.

15 | Conclusion

Researching and writing this book has made me realize just how much a teacher has to think about. Planning, preparing, providing and monitoring the education of large numbers of students. Helping these students to develop as a group, but treating them as individuals. Ensuring their safety and well-being throughout the school day. Teaching them to communicate effectively, act responsibly and treat others with respect. Challenging them. Inspiring them. Motivating them. Finding a way for each of them to reach their full potential, no matter where they have started from. And all of this before I've even mentioned behaviour management . . .

Getting to grips with challenging behaviour requires a considerable amount of input. For successful results, it needs to be dealt with diligently and consistently. However, spending time on behaviour issues can liberate your classroom in other ways. If you are on top of behaviour, you may find you are able to be more adventurous in your overall approach, able to push your students harder and able to enjoy more of those 'this makes it all worth it' moments.

Some may find behaviour management comes naturally, others may have to work at it; but with practice and patience, effective techniques can be developed and mastered. Tackling low-level issues and focusing on preventative steps may mean fewer or no major difficulties. Endeavouring to show students respect, empathy and encouragement can help them to overcome their own negative preconceptions about themselves and their schooling. Establishing a voice that is firm and assertive, but avoids negative confrontation, will present you as a respectable, strong and confident leader. And on the occasional day when it does all get a bit much, remember, you're only human! Good luck . . .

Appendix: Causes of disruptive behaviour checklist

General issues

- Lack of awareness or respect for boundaries: consistent boundary-setting not established in the home.
- Lack of motivation to learn: education not valued within the home or social environment.
- Unresolved emotional issues: for example, anger, resentment or jealousy, leading to aggressive, disruptive behaviour.
- Under-developed communication skills: inability to articulate or express thoughts and feelings effectively, leading to frustrated behaviour.
- Unfulfilled physiological needs: lack of sleep (a common problem), lack of nutritious food.

Learning issues

- Low self-esteem regarding learning resulting in work refusal or avoidance.
- Unidentified learning needs.
- Level of challenge inappropriate to individual learning ability: too difficult, too easy, too 'boring'.
- Pacing of tasks: student has too much or too little time to complete work.
- Confusion: lack of understanding of instructions or of what is required from a task.

Socialization issues

- Low self-esteem regarding socialization, leading to behaviours that aggravate or wind others up.
- Low self-esteem leading to desire to prove self-worth through dominating or intimidating others (including teachers!).

- Peer recognition: seeking attention from other students, making them laugh, gaining 'respect', living up to a reputation.
- Unresolved issues from previous lesson/breaktime.

Teacher–student relationship issues

- Student seeking attention from adults: placing excessive demands on teacher time.
- Perceived injustice: student feels they have been treated unfairly or behavioural difficulties are inconsistently dealt with.
- Teacher too 'soft': student feels they have nothing to lose by misbehaving.
- Teacher too 'strict': student perceives teacher as unpleasant, or unreasonable, leading to lack of motivation to cooperate.
- Student feels 'labelled': if they are going to blamed for everything anyway, what have they go to lose . . .
- Lack of positive reinforcement: absence of praise or encouragement leading to low morale.

Index